The

"Whether you're searching for more meaning and joy in your life or helping others discover and live their best lives, using The Passion Principle book makes a world of difference. It'll help you create rich personal treasure maps using the landmark discoveries of positive psychology along with the powerful processes developed by Bruce and Randy, both experienced therapists and coaches. You'll read fascinating stories about the challenges and triumphs of well-known celebrities as well as everyday people, all on the quest to live and sustain lives of greater passion and purpose. Living the Passion Principle will serve you and humanity."
Marci Shimoff, #1 NY Times bestselling author, Happy for No Reason, Love for No Reason and Chicken Soup for the Woman's Soul, Featured teacher in The Secret

"As a therapist, I have encountered clients searching and yearning for more excitement, involvement, and passion in life – yet without a sense of how to accomplish that. The authors have written a book with invaluable guidance and insights on how to move your life in a more passionate direction. Let The Passion Principle be your personal guide for discovering your passion."
Jacqueline Doyle
Psychologist, Former president of the Humanistic Psychology Association

"The Passion Principle is a great tool for helping you or your clients discover and live your passions! When asked, I have always been able to tell others what my current passions are. However, after completing core exercises in the Passion Principle which help readers list their past, present, and future passions, I was able to identify the common threads that exist in all three realms. The exercise helped me

remember the delights I had as a child and adolescent and then link them to my present and future endeavors in a new and meaningful way. I highly recommend this book for those of you who are seeking to bring your whole and passionate self into your life and relationships."

Elaine Casquarelli, Licensed Mental Health Counselor

The Passion Principle:

How to Love Your Most Passionate Life

Bruce Hutchison, PhD

and

Randy Crutcher, EdD

OTHER BOOKS BY BRUCE HUTCHISON

The Shakespeare Conspiracy: A Clayton Lovell Stone Adventure

The Queen and the Playwright: Love's Labor Lost

Body of Evidence: The Adventure of a Lifetime

Bruce's Website:
www.readbrucebooks.com
Contact: readbrucebooks@gmail.com

OTHER PUBLICATIONS BY RANDY CRUTCHER

Divine Dog Wisdom Cards and Guidebook by Randy Crutcher and Barb Horn

Cosmic Cat Wisdom Cards and Guidebook by Randy Crutcher and Barb Horn

Randy's Website:
www.quantumleapcoaching.org

Published in the United States, by EnlightenUp LLC, Colorado

ISBN 978-0-692-08782-4

Cover design by Rachel Lopez

OTHER BOOKS BY BRUCE HUTCHISON

The Shakespeare Conspiracy: A Clayton Lovell Stone Adventure

The Romanov Conspiracy: A Clayton Lovell Stone Adventure

The Queen and the Playwright: Love's Labor Lost

Body of Evidence: The Adventure of a Lifetime

Bruce's Website: **www.readbrucebooks.com**

RANDY CRUTCHER'S BLOG AND CONTACT

Website: **www.quantumleapcoaching.org**

Blogsite: **www.everymansblog.net**

DEDICATION

Bruce wants to thank his wife Nancy for her support and encouragement, and for her constant love that flows easily and naturally. He also wants to thank all the patients and therapy clients he has had over the years. As much as he has helped them, they have shown him how to overcome struggles and obstacles to continually discover and rediscover passions in his own life.

Randy would like to dedicate this book to his parents Ellen M. Crutcher and Dr. Thomas Wallace Crutcher, both lifelong educators and role models who lived their passions professionally, socially, creatively and recreationally all of their adult lives. At the writing of this book Randy's dad Tom, at 92 years of age, is still living his passions and encouraging the work of spreading passion globally. And this book would not be possible without the love, support and contribution of Dr. Karin Lubin, Randy's lifelong partner in all their shared passions.

TABLE OF CONTENTS

Why The Passion Principle?
Foreword by Janet Bray Attwood

If you've picked up this book or if someone laid it in your hands, chances are it's because you're ready for more excitement, joy, and sense of purpose in your life. But it's more likely that you feel something is missing in your life; you may be trudging through your days, hoping or waiting for something better to come your way.

If you do feel a certain emptiness or missing element, you're not alone. Gallup and Harris polls indicate that a majority of us are less engaged, fulfilled, and productive than we would like to be. Suicide, addiction, and violence are on the rise. Gangs and terrorist organizations seek vulnerable recruits by offering a false and distorted promise of power and purpose. What we truly need is a deeper sense of personal purpose and passion directed toward creativity, compassion, and connection with ourselves and with others in the world.

Years before my coauthor, Chris Attwood, and I began thinking about writing The Passion Test: The Effortless Path to Discovering Your Life Purpose, we both sensed the power of passion as a deeply motivating force. Through trial and error, we discovered—sometimes painfully—that being clear about what we want drives a sense of purpose that fills life with energy and stamina for the dance along life's path. When our life is filled with passion and purpose, our days brighten and we step lighter. We see our goal on the horizon and feel fulfilled and joyful as we step toward it, always remembering to stop and smell the roses along the way. We are unstoppable when it comes to living our passions and helping others do the same.

Years of experience—and now the experiences of thousands of others—have reinforced what we wrote about in The Passion Test, which became an immediate New York Times best seller and remained in the top one hundred in Amazon self-help books for years thereafter. Since then, it has become even clearer that passion is everyone's birthright—that the tools to discover, live, and sustain passion can be taught, mastered, and practiced. They can be lived fully day to day.

So why do we need another book about passion? The Passion Test is still out there, still being read, and still being taught in four dozen countries around the world. The Passion Test is still the foundation of the Passion Test principles. But since we wrote The Passion Test, a lot has been discovered that supports and adds to that foundation. Psychological research has developed additional proven methods to supplement and sustain the clarity and direction that Chris and I describe in The Passion Test, and which hundreds of Passion Test facilitators now teach worldwide.

It doesn't matter so much where you begin. You could begin by reading The Passion Test or by participating in one of the Passion Test workshops given around the world. Or you could begin by reading this book, The Passion Principle, which has fascinating stories about people finding and living their passions plus concrete steps for broadening and deepening your own passions.

The Passion Principle can be considered a true companion volume to The Passion Test, as it expands one's knowledge while supporting the passion journey in a powerful and engaging way. As I have shared with the coauthors, Bruce Hutchison and Randy Crutcher, I am excited about the possibility of collaborating with a growing number of psychologists, therapists, educators, social workers, and anyone else who sees passion as a key element in helping others achieve their full potential. I am happy to work with so many wonderful people who serve so many others on a daily basis, bringing them proven knowledge of what connects people to their dreams, hopes, and passions.

So whether you're looking for a reliable guide for your personal passion journey or you're a professional looking to facilitate someone else's discovery, it's my hope that you use The Passion Principle to actively engage in an ongoing process of discovering, living, and sustaining your passions, and that you spread joy and passion in your own sphere of life.

To Your Most Passionate Life and Success!
Janet Bray Attwood

Introduction

Martha Rathtower said she was tired of her life. She said she'd had it up to here, holding a still finger across her neck just beneath her chin to silently express that if she had to endure one more inch of suffering, she'd either suffocate or drown. She'd already endured a left-breast radical mastectomy. After painful radiation and chemotherapy, she discovered another lump in her right breast and lost that to the surgeon's knife.

Less than a year later, just when life seemed to be getting back to normal, her skin started itching with what she called a constant "creepy-crawly" sensation. "Oh my god," she thought. "It's back again."

But it wasn't back again. Another enemy had invaded her. As if cancer hadn't been enough, now she was diagnosed with Morgellons disease, a rare skin disorder characterized by itching, skin sores, fatigue, visual disturbances, slow memory loss, and an inability to concentrate. She was devastated and desperate to learn everything she could about this condition. When she searched online she found there was very little to learn, although she did find others who felt isolated, desperate, and alone.

Angry at the incredible unfairness of her malaise, she suddenly had a burst of energy and swung into action. She started an online group and arranged to meet whomever she could, anyone she could manage to get to by car. Her small group soon became fast friends. They supported each other. They were on constant call in the middle of the night when depression hit and an understanding friend was needed to keep it at bay.

Martha later told us, "I not only regained my energy, but once I met the others and got beyond my anger, I felt passionate about whatever I could do. Oddly, I felt more alive than ever. Now I had something to do. Something to care about. Something that meant something. I wanted to live more than ever, be as healthy as I could. But it wasn't the Morgellons disease that kick-started me into a passionate life. It was a passion for helping and healing that I never felt before. I can't thank the Morgellons disease, but I am grateful for what it gave me."

Trudy Gonzales had led a charmed life, at least after a few rough spots in the beginning. With a working-class family struggling to make ends meet but dedicated to her success, she'd excelled in school, worked for a while in the hospitality industry, fell in love with and married a man with a well-paying job, and had three beautiful children.

Despite all this, she began to wonder if this was all there was to life. And what would she do when the kids got older and didn't need her anymore? She had skills; she was a dedicated volunteer at her children's school. In other words, she was the über–soccer mom.

Some days Trudy felt a bit like she was in a gilded cage. All the comforts, but where was the challenge? How could she begin to reclaim those skills and abilities she'd used in her career before she'd had a family and still make it work for who and where she was now? More than that, how could she tap into the even deeper sense of joy, satisfaction, meaning, and purpose that she suspected might still be possible for her?

Jeff DeLorme felt as if he'd hit a major dead end in his life. With long commutes and hours to match, he'd not been happy for some time. Away from Alicia, his nine-year-old daughter, and Devon, his thirteen-year-old son, for way too much of the day and week, he felt torn between career and family. And his passion for his career had ebbed as it had become more about the paycheck than anything else. He was dying inside.

Jeff knew something had to give. He just couldn't see himself continuing to run the rat race when so much of his bucket list had not been fulfilled—when so much of what was really important had been neglected. He wondered what would make him truly happy and what would help him get back the energy, excitement, and love of life he'd once had.

Martha, Trudy, and Jeff were each asking, "What is my purpose in life? What is my passion? Where do I go from here?" They were all struggling to create a more fulfilling life that better fit their hopes, dreams, and desires. They were searching for a life of greater passion. Maybe you are as well. Aren't we all?

Can you imagine what it would be like to live your life with greater passion? Passion infuses life with pleasure, purpose, and meaning. It spurs energy, directs vision, and jolts you out of bed in the morning—excited, involved, and ready to go. It's the master key to unlocking personal and business success: when you love what you do, you do your best. And it's infectious. Others see your drive and want to follow you.

Passion is natural. It's embedded in you, awaiting discovery, rediscovery, or renewal. As author and lecturer Joseph Campbell said in one of his PBS conversations with Bill Moyers, "If you follow your bliss [passion], you put yourself on a kind of track that has been there all the while." Based on recent research in the field of positive psychology, The Passion Principle offers a road map for uncovering and unleashing the authentic power of your true passionate self.

Is This Book for You?

The Passion Principle is for anyone who "gets" that understanding and developing your passions is a direct path to living a good life. It's for anyone interested in the field of positive psychology. It's also for anyone who thinks that self-help is great—as long as there's science behind it. Research on the topic of passion abounds, and we're going to share it with you in this book.

The Passion Principle can be used by psychologists, educators, workshop leaders, and certified Passion Test facilitators throughout the world. The bottom line is this: If you or your clients/students want more out of life, then this book is for you.

The Original Passion Test

What's that Passion Test thing we just mentioned? It's a test created by Janet Attwood, coauthor with Chris Attwood of the New York Times best seller The Passion Test, which for some of you was your introduction to working with your passions.

The Passion Principle is a companion volume to The Passion Test. It's not necessary for you to have read or worked with The Passion Test, but for those of you haven't yet read it, here's a summary of the original Passion Test.

Those who take the Passion Test spend quiet time visualizing their ideal life. They consider their ideal life at work and in their relationships: their most desirable living arrangements, creative projects, recreation, service to others, hopes, dreams, and (for some) spiritual development. After a review of these life categories, they develop a working list of passions. From that list, they engage in a powerful prioritization process designed to get people out of their heads and into their hearts to discover what would truly make them happy and content. They end up with a list of their current top five passions.

The passion descriptions on that list are affirmative, inspirational, present-tense statements that provide a sense of what it would feel like if they were already there, already living their passions. They then score their passions somewhere on a scale of 0 to 10, with 0 signifying that a passion is not showing up in their lives at all right now and 10 indicating that it's showing up a great deal. This gives them a baseline from which to begin a new journey to living more of their passions.

After scoring their passions, the next step in the Passion Test is to create passion markers. Different from goals, markers are the milestones or evidence that the Passion Test takers would need to see to convince them that they are fully living a particular passion. As Janet and Chris write in The Passion Test, "What we put our attention on grows stronger in our lives." Markers direct people's attention toward inspired action steps that they can take to begin living a passion or living it more fully.

If, for example, one of your top five passion statements is "I am healthy, vital, strong, and sexy!" you would create markers that, once reached, would convince you that you were making progress in achieving that passion. One marker might be "I jump out of bed in the morning excited and ready to begin my day." Another might be "People frequently tell me I'm glowing and that they want what I'm having!"

Like life itself, passion markers are always a work in progress. As you move closer to realizing a passion marker, you may think of other markers that lead you further forward or sometimes lead you to change direction. Thoughts or ideas may emerge that are entirely different from what you initially thought, sometimes even bigger and better than you could have imagined. The key is to keep thinking big, writing your ideas down and keeping your attention engaged by taking action aligned with your passions.

What You'll Find in This Book

The Passion Principle chapters that follow will extend and deepen any passion work you may already have done using the Passion Test. If you have taken the Passion Test, keep the most current list of your top five passions handy, along with your most recent passion markers. If you haven't read or taken the Passion Test, that's OK; the guides and exercises in The Passion Principle will be your starting point on the exciting path to discovering your passions.

In Part I, "Discovering Your Passions," you'll be invited to assess your personal passion potential. Passion will be defined in a personal, practical, and measurable way. You'll then be asked to complete an exercise that will help you delve into dozens of potential passions from your past, present, and anticipated future. Finally, you'll be guided to develop a Personal Passion Action Plan and learn about and weigh the factors relevant to successfully implementing that plan.

In Part II, "Living Your Passions," you'll learn how to overcome obstacles to living your passions and gain more insight into how to more fully live your passions in your relationships, your work, and your life in general.

In Part III, "Sustaining Your Passions," you'll gain a fuller understanding of how the practice of savoring, being in flow, gratitude, and seeking ever deeper meaning support you in continuing to live more passionately, even in the face of changing conditions and circumstances.

The concluding chapters underscore the vital reasons for discovering, acting on, deepening, and sustaining your personal passions. They also detail the impact that your personal passions can have on the world. Included are forms that will help you discover and activate your passions, as well as a chapter-by-chapter reference section providing a more detailed description of the research underlying The Passion Principle procedures and exercises.

While you can use the charts and exercise questionnaires in this book as you come to them, we recommend that you use a notebook or create a computer file to record and save your answers to the exercise questions, for both immediate use and later reflection. That way, you'll always have fresh templates you can reuse as your passion journey progresses.

By the time you finish reading this book and completing the exercises, we expect—and this is backed up by more than a decade of psychological research and the authors' combined experience teaching passion workshops—that you will have more excitement, adventure, and passion in your life!

Part I: Discovering Your Passions

"When you are clear, what you choose to have show up in your life, will—and only to the extent you are clear."

Janet Bray Attwood

CHAPTER 1

Got Passion?

All strivings for growth and self-discovery begin at a starting point and aim toward a desirable goal. The results of your passion discovery efforts should be meaningful and measurable—and we begin this book by giving you a tool to help you get started on your passion journey.

The self-assessment with the following Passion Start Up Score places a stake at the beginning of your journey so you can easily see and measure your progress, both along the way and at the end. Six self-assessment passion questions—each self-rated on a scale of 1 ("Don't agree") to 7 ("Strongly agree")—will determine your starting point. A reassessment at the end of your journey will measure how far you've come.

This beginning rating is just for you, so answer as honestly as you can. Your overall score and individual scores may be low at the start—that's expected. It's only a start. When you rate yourself again at the end of the last chapter, you'll be amazed at your progress. You will have come a long way.

In this chapter, we'll also begin to introduce some of the research on passion and talk about how to apply it to make a meaningful difference in your life. After all, we believe that everyone wants to live more than just an "OK" life.

Now turn to the next page and test yourself.

Passion Startup Score

Right now, at the beginning of this journey, I feel . . . (write your answer)

Now use the following scale to answer the questions below:

Don't Agree			Mostly Agree		Strongly Agree	
1	2	3	4	5	6	7

I have put a lot of thought into the personal meaning of passion.

1 2 3 4 5 6 7

I am aware of five specific ways to increase passion in my life.

1 2 3 4 5 6 7

I am confident I can feel more alive and passionate in the future.

1 2 3 4 5 6 7

I am aware of a long list of passions that I could add to my life.

1 2 3 4 5 6 7

I know the procedures to take to define my passions more clearly.

1 2 3 4 5 6 7

I have already begun to increase passion in my life in one or more ways.

1 2 3 4 5 6 7

Beginning Passion Score = (add total scores) ☐

To live a life filled with passion sounds simple: find your passion and follow it. But that's like saying that the way to get rich is to make money or that the road to happiness is satisfaction. The questions you'd probably ask in these instances are, how do you make money and where does the road to satisfaction begin?

Remember as a child how passionate and excited you were about nearly everything—a ladybug crawling up a tree, the shape of a cloud floating across a blue sky, that first day at the pool, or dashing under a cool lawn sprinkler? Whatever happened to that innate excitement, passion, and vitality? Why does it take so much more to stimulate an adult's awe and wonder? Why do some of us hold on to more passion than others as we grow? Is there a way to recapture that childlike exuberance and high-spirited enthusiasm and make it part of our everyday life? Italian film director Federico Fellini was once quoted as saying, "There is no end. There is no beginning. There is only an infinite passion for life." Infinite passion? Wouldn't it be great if we all had that?

Ask yourself why you are reading this book. It's probably because you have an interest in passion and because you'd like to feel more passion in your life, to really live it and sustain it. You may be one of those that Henry David Thoreau speaks of in his famous quote, "'Most men lead lives of quiet desperation." You'd probably like to discover an effective way to discover and generate more passion—right?

There are racks of library shelves filled with books on motivation and on how to live a happy life, and quite a few on the specific topic of passion. If you google the word passion, you come up with seven million hits in .25 seconds. If you research book titles containing the word passion on Amazon.com, you're offered a choice of twelve thousand books in paperback and four thousand in hardback. Of course, a lot of those are romance novels, but that's still a lot of interest in passion!

Stumbling onto Happiness

After journalist Malcolm Gladwell (author of Blink, The Tipping Point, and Outliers) reviewed Dan Gilbert's bestselling book, Stumbling on Happiness, he happened to be sitting next to Gilbert on a flight from New York to California. He described Gilbert as a man with a shiny bald head and irrepressible good humor. They immediately struck up a conversation that carried them from takeoff at JFK, across the Mississippi and the Rockies, and all the way to LAX in Los Angeles.

According to Gladwell, Gilbert's Stumbling on Happiness "is about a very simple but powerful idea. What distinguishes us as human beings from other animals is our ability to predict the future—or rather, our interest in predicting the future. We often attempt to be happy by trying to exert some control over our futures. But by any objective measure, we are really bad at that predictive function. We're terrible at knowing how we will feel a day, or a month, or a year from now, and even worse at knowing what will and will not bring us that cherished happiness."

Psychologists have little interest in stumbling onto happiness or in predicting the future. We do have an interest in studying what can be done right now, in the present, to increase the frequency, duration, and quality of happiness. Like most clinical psychologists, Bruce Hutchison (coauthor of this book) is interested in applying the psychological research gleaned over the past decade in ways that actually make a difference in people's lives.

Dream Chasers

Passion often amounts to discovering and pursuing your dreams. Management consultants and inspirational gurus, along with many authors and poets, frequently advise, "Don't bother chasing success. Follow your dreams and success will follow you." A lesser known quote by Henry David Thoreau tells us, "Live the life you imagine. Go confidently in the direction of your dreams." Poet and artist Pamela Vaull Starr said it this way: "Dream deep, for every dream precedes a goal."

Therapy clients often hope to find a passion to fill a void or a nagging emptiness in life, a relationship, or a marriage. One young man, just starting his adult life, said, "I'm not sure what I want to do, but I want to be excited. I want to feel good about it." Another woman in her mid-thirties said, "I know I have more inside me. There's something holding me back. I want to break through that barrier and discover what's on the other side." Sherry, a recently divorced thirty-six-year-old X-ray technician, told Bruce as soon as she sat down on the therapy couch, "I think I can get back to being OK again, but I'm wondering if 'OK' is enough."

Most of us lead a life that's at least OK, but we

sometimes wonder if it could be better than that; could we feel more engaged and passionate in what we do and where we're going? Sometimes it's a feeling that something's missing, put so well in the lyrics of Peggy Lee's seventies hit, "Is That All There Is?" Those lyrics go:

When I was 12 years old, my father took me to the circus, the greatest show on earth.

There were clowns and elephants and dancing bears.

And a beautiful lady in pink tights flew high above our heads.

And as I sat there watching the marvelous spectacle,I had the feeling that something was missing.

I don't know what, but when it was over, I said to myself,

'Is that all there is to a circus?'

And then the chorus and constant refrain after a lost relationship and after every other life experience…

Is that all there is?
If that's all there is, my friends,
Then let's keep dancing.
Let's break out the booze and have a ball,
If that's all there is.

But an alcoholic escape and partying are only temporary and illusionary fixes for boredom, low-level depression, or just plain "I wish there were more to my life." Expecting a circus, or a marriage, or a career to add meaning and passion to your life may be expecting more than these elements have to offer— unless that particular circus or marriage or career is motivated by a passion that springs from somewhere deep inside. It can only fill that void you feel when it comes from within you because it must be your passion changing you as you grow and evolve from who you are to who you can be.

But how exactly can you follow Thoreau's advice and live the life you imagine? How do you reach for a dream, pull it down from the clouds, anchor it on solid earth, and find a path that can lead you to its fulfillment? How do you hitch that dream to your passions, and how do you know which actions to take that will lead you ever onward down that path?

The dreams and passions of those advancing the field of positive psychology for the last decade have been to develop and test methods to do just that. Psychologists have tested passion discovery techniques in ordinary life and in the toughest of places—prisons, for example—knowing that if it works within those walls and limitations, it should work where possibilities are wider and life is easier.

Even in Prison

Dr. Joe Hatcher, a correctional psychologist Bruce admires, works in a medium security prison in Oshkosh, Wisconsin. In an online article at Corrections.com entitled "Positive Psychology and Incarceration: Can You Promote Positive Emotion in Inmates and Staff?" Dr. Hatcher writes: "Positive Psychology is easy to use in groups because it offers a number of 'homework' exercises that can be completed outside of the group and then be shared in group meetings."

The actor Robert Downey Jr., who has been in more jails and rehabs than some of the prisoners Bruce has worked with, once said in an interview, "I think I've been lucky. My frequent appearances on Court TV have brought to me another level than just the actor guy." Downey's comment, referring to his drug and alcohol addictions, led Bruce to think about how our circumstances, conditions, and learning imprison us. If inmates can learn to think outside the boundaries of their physical and mental prison, how can the rest of us discover and nurture passions that go beyond the bounds of our own limited thinking?

Dr. Hatcher's prison work was based on a well-known and validated positive psychology experiment known as Three Good Things. In that study, it turned out that when people simply noticed good things during the day, the result was noticing more the next day and the next day after that. The cumulative effect increased gratitude and appreciation and supported the notion that the more you love and feel passionate about something, the more you actively surround yourself with good things to notice and appreciate. In one of the passion discovery exercises in this book, you'll explore ways to increase gratitude and appreciation in order to have and sustain more of what you want in your life.

As screenwriter and Director Joss Whedon observed, "Passion lies in all of us, sleeping, waiting. It stirs us, opens its jaws, and howls. It speaks to us. It guides us. What other choice do we have? Without passion, we'd be truly dead." If passion is the spirit and energy that stirs and guides us, how can we listen more closely and more often? How can we let it speak and guide us? That's what the rest of this book is about.

CHAPTER 2

What Is Passion, Anyway?

Before you do any more exercises, let's take a moment to talk about the nature of passion. What exactly is passion?

Well, when someone asks, "What are you passionate about?" you usually know something about what they mean: What do you feel strongly about? What do you love? What activities do you enjoy? What is most important and meaningful to you?

Those are all pretty good definitions of passion, but when a psychologist studies a subject, the first thing he or she does is precisely define the phenomenon in operational terms so that other researchers know exactly what is meant and can replicate the results in subsequent studies. That sort of replication is the scientific method in a nutshell.

Positive psychology has some fascinating things to tell us about passion, and we'll share those with you in this chapter. We'll start by defining passion—and what makes something a passion rather than just a means to an end. We'll describe the self-defining nature of passion—things that reveal our passions to us. We'll also tell you about the birth of positive psychology and its interest in passion, as well as something called your passion set point, which explores the question of whether it's really possible to increase your passion for life.

Even if you're not enthralled with definitions and set points—if you just want to get on with the process of discovering your passions—we think you'll find it interesting to see what prominent researchers say about passion. Their insights could give you a basis for figuring out whether something is your passion or not. So we recommend that before you jump into the exercises in the next chapter, take a look at things we talk about here, which may help you in examining your own passions further.

Passion Defined

Psychologist Robert Vallerand at the University of Quebec at Montreal has been one of the leading researchers on the topic of passion. Vallerand defines passion as a strong inclination toward an activity that has the following four qualities:

It's something a person strongly likes or loves.

It's a central part of someone's self-definition—of what they consider themselves to be.

It's something the individual feels is of value to herself and others.

It's an activity that someone devotes a good deal of time and energy to.

The Passion Test book defines passion this way: "Your passions are those things that you love and care about most, those things that when your life is connected to them, you feel passionate." We like this definition, as it makes the connection between activities and psychological states of being, both of which are measurable—measurability being another criterion for working within the scientific method.

We'll be working with these defined aspects of passion throughout The Passion Principle, and we'll show you exactly how you can measurably increase your passion in and for your life.

Passion as a Self-Defining Activity

When you find yourself at a party or in a group of strangers and someone approaches you and says, "Hello. I'm (they give their name); who are you?" you usually give him your name. If the stranger wants to take the next step to get to know you, his next question is usually "What do you do?"—by which he means, "What's your profession, your job?" That knowledge tells him something about your education and income level, what your interests are likely to be, what lifestyle you probably live—and in general terms, whether or not the two of you might have something in common. In short, your answer to "What do you do?" tells someone a lot about you.

If that introduction hurdle is surmounted and the stranger is still interested, his next question might be, "What do you like to do?" He wants to know if your interests and passions are the same as his, if what you do resonates with him, if there might be a common interest to discuss, or at least if yours are ones he could relate to, admire, or learn something about. He wants to know what you love to do and what you spend a fair amount of time doing, to which you might respond, "I like to read," "I'm a big football fan," or "I love movies." He might then respond, "I like to read too," or "I go to the movies every chance I get," or "I'm a Giants fan myself."

Christopher Peterson, a prominent researcher in positive psychology, sees our underlying passions as a major way we define ourselves and a continuing motivation for choosing our future direction. In his textbook, A Primer in Positive Psychology (2006), Peterson writes, "We all have interests and passions that partially define who we are." He goes on to say that for some, passions involve recreational activities like snow skiing, softball, or bridge. For others, passions or callings involve work and career. Others feel passionate about spending time with family and loved ones. Still others are passionate about a pet, reading romance novels, listening to National Public Radio, or devouring the New York Times every Sunday. If our passions constitute an important part of who we are and how we express our unique individuality, then a key component of living a good life is understanding, developing, and engaging our passions to the greatest extent we can.

Peterson tells the story of his friend Jack, a married high school teacher with two children, who played second base in high school and who continues to play second base as an adult on a local softball team. When Jack is introduced to a stranger who asks what he does, he invariably answers, "I play second base." It's almost as if someone had asked him, "Who are you?" and he answered, "I'm a second-baseman. That's who I am." Obviously, being a second-baseman is not all Jack is, does, or feels passionate about, but that's the chest badge he points to.

Peterson believes that Jack's pride in playing second base partly emanates from an innate, millennia-old human desire to master the environment. Since the human brain is a problem-solving mechanism, it takes inherent pleasure in doing what it's designed to do: learning and figuring out what it has to do to create and survive. Jack feels good about his baseball achievements because he has mastered them.

Peterson points to other examples of mastery: a young child who delights in learning to walk and then giggles with pride as he or she finally balances and moves upright across the living room floor, or an older child who is thrilled to learn to ride a two-wheel bike when that bike stops wobbling and suddenly rolls evenly down the street, or a computer-illiterate adult who initially learns to double-click an email and send it off into cyberspace with that wonderful whooshing sound. There are external rewards for learning all these skills, but Peterson feels that there is an innate, internal satisfaction in the mastery itself and that this is particularly true of passions, which are pursued purely for the inherent joy people experience from them.

Since passions constitute a central part of how people define themselves, people often form close relationships with others who share, support, and encourage their passions, and they often use their shared passions as a basis for those relationships.

Love and Value

One of the markers that Vallerand uses to define an activity as a passion is that the activity is "strongly liked or loved." It is certainly possible to participate in an activity that partially defines you ("I am a lawyer," or "I play golf.") but that you no longer like or love. You may have grown tired of the law and are now simply hanging in there until you've saved enough for retirement and a chance to move to the Bahamas. Or you may have taken up golf because you're a salesperson or a lobbyist who needs to be out on the links to network with potential customers or clients. In both cases, you may value the activity—in one case for the salary, in the other for the connections—and you may identify yourself as lawyer or golfer, but you may neither love nor especially like golf or the law. You're simply using them as a means to an end. They're not passions.

The Time Factor

Another marker that Vallerand uses to define an activity as a passion is that the activity is one in which you spend a good deal of time. For our purposes—for exploring, discovering, and developing your personal passions—we will consider Vallerand's time component as tentative. Here's why: You may have one or more passions that you love and value, that you're strongly inclined toward, and that you feel are a central part of you ("I've always loved to play the piano" or "I've been trying to perfect my tennis serve") but that you don't currently spend much time doing or paying attention to.

A soldier deployed overseas, for example, may be unable to feed the pets she loves and trained because her deployment doesn't allow it. Or she may have once collected old coins and still considers herself to be an avid collector, even though she doesn't spend nearly the time on coin collecting that she once did. She may think that being spiritual is central to who she is, although she's not currently meditating regularly or engaging in what she considers spiritual practice. By Vallerand's definition, none of these activities would be considered a passion because they don't meet the "considerable amount of time" requirement.

In those cases, we would consider coin collecting, animal training, and being spiritual to be dormant passions since they meet Vallerand's other criteria: a strong inclination toward a self-defining activity ("I am a coin collector" or "I train dogs" or "I meditate") that is still loved and valued. Collecting, dog training, and meditating are passions that are simply waiting in the wings, perhaps to be recalled onstage at some later point.

Some passions require less time than others—the nature

of the passion itself may limit the time required to pursue it. It could be argued that some women are passionate about dressing and applying makeup. They thoroughly enjoy the process and consider fashion, dressing, and makeup an important part of their image and persona. The activity fits all the requirements of Vallerand's passion definition with the exception that the activity itself is usually time limited, given how long it takes to dress and sit in front of a mirror.

Bruce loves to soak in the hot tub on his back deck in Santa Fe and view the night sky. He hops in that tub four or five nights a week, leans back, and watches the stars. He considers himself a "hot-tubber." He loves it. But twenty minutes is all his body can stand. He feels passionate about hot-tubbing despite the limited time he spends viewing the night sky immersed in hot water.

Both of Bruce's parents considered themselves lapidaries. For years, they were passionate about finding, cutting, and polishing semiprecious stones. After they retired and moved, they carted along their diamond-tipped table saw, grinders, and polishers, and they had the movers maneuver all their heavy rocks and equipment into a corner basement room devoted to cutting and polishing. They plugged in their machines, hooked up a water line to the diamond saw, and then spent the next several years watching their equipment gather dust under the clear plastic cover Bruce's mother had draped across it. They never spent another minute on a hobby that had previously occupied hours, days, and sometimes weeks of their time—traveling out West to find stones in New Mexico and Arizona. They still considered themselves "rock hounds" and enjoyed showing their collection off to guests, although they no longer sought stones or cut and polished a single surface.

By Vallerand's strict definition, rock hunting and polishing would not be a passion for Bruce's parents because it no longer filled the "considerable amount of time" requirement. Yet their strong enthusiasm for displaying, viewing, and bragging about their hobby remained. It was still a passion.

As you discover, uncover, or rediscover passions, consider the time element the least of your considerations if a potential passion meets the other three parts of Vallerand's passion definition.

Psychology's Passionate New Direction

When and why did psychologists get interested in passion? The wind in psychology's passion sails shifted dramatically in the spring of 2000 when Martin Seligman (considered a founder of positive psychology) and Mihaly Csikszentmihalyi—aka Marti and Mike—wrote a joint article in which they argued, "We believe that a psychology of positive human functioning will arise which achieves a scientific understanding and effective interventions to build thriving individuals, families, and communities."

Prior to that groundbreaking article, clinical psychologists were primarily interested in diagnosing and treating mental illness—helping clients regain normal function more than making interventions to "build thriving individuals." But Marti and Mike's own passion to help people achieve more than just a cure for mental illness encouraged many of us to reconsider that uplifting possibility.

The positive psychology movement and the interventions it spurred quickly took hold when Marti was invited to define the emerging field. He wrote: "Positive psychology is an umbrella term for the study of positive emotions, positive character traits, and enabling institutions. Research findings from positive psychology are intended to supplement, not remotely to replace, what is known about human suffering, weakness, and disorder. The intent is to have a more complete and balanced scientific understanding of the human experience—the peaks, the valleys, and everything in between. We believe that a complete science and a complete practice of psychology should include an understanding of suffering and happiness, as well as their interaction, and validated interventions that both relieve suffering and increase happiness—two separable endeavors."

But what are those validated interventions? What methods have been shown to be the most effective and how do you choose among them? In considering that, Mike wrote in the same article cited above, "Contrary to what most of us believe, happiness does not simply happen. It's something that we make happen."

But how do we make it happen? And what part does passion play in happiness? Much has been learned about that in the years since Marti and Mike's initial American Psychologist article.

William Compton described psychology's new direction as "making normal life more fulfilling." Instead of simply helping the depressed or anxious achieve normalcy, a good cause in itself, the new positive psychology would consider "normal"—that is, the absence of mental health symptoms—as merely a foundation on which to build. The goal is no longer normalcy. The bar has been raised.

The new goal is achieving a full, thriving, passionate potential. Someone who has achieved this goal is described by Mike as "someone whose aliveness and spirit are expressed not only in personal productivity and activity, but whose infectious energy infuses those with which they come in contact." One of the positive emotions that Marti, Mike, and others have studied is passion—sometimes called zest or vitality for life.

Effective Passion Interventions

In one randomly assigned control-group study, Marti tested "five purported happiness interventions and one plausible control exercise." In discussing his results, Marti stated that "we found that three of the interventions lastingly increased happiness and decreased depressive symptoms" and that "two of the exercises—(1) using signature strengths in a new way and (2) the "three good things" exercise—increased happiness and decreased depressive symptoms over a six-month period."

In the "three good things in life" intervention, Marti said, "participants were asked to write down three things that went well each day every night for one week. In addition, they were asked to provide a causal explanation for each 'good thing.'"

Part of the reason the "three good things" intervention worked was that it required participants to focus on what happened that day that was good and then consider what they may have done to create or facilitate those good things. As the authors say in The Passion Test book, "What you put your attention on grows stronger in your life." They also say that the purpose of action and activity is that it keeps your attention on your passions. In other words, doing more of what you enjoy and love, then noticing what happened as a result, strengthens that passion.

When those in the experiment recognized the part they played in making good things happen, they deliberately placed themselves in "good-happening environments," which made it more likely that good things would happen while they were there. In the passion discovery exercises in the next chapter, you will learn what your passions are and in what situations you're more likely to experience them.

Passion and Character Strengths

In Marti's second successful experimental intervention—the "using signature strengths in a new way" exercise—subjects were asked to complete an online Character Strengths Inventory (the VIA Survey of Character Strengths at AuthenticHappiness.com) in order to identify their top five character strengths from a possible list of twenty-one. They were then asked to use one of their top five strengths in a new and different way every day for one week.

This character strengths intervention guided participants to better understand and apply their underlying character strengths in new and different ways that added to their satisfaction and to the overall quality of their lives. Coauthor Randy has noticed in his own life and work with clients that when you take action that is in alignment with who you really are, your satisfaction is guaranteed to increase.

The VIA Survey of Character Strengths Inventory is available to take free at the University of Pennsylvania's webpage AuthenticHappiness.com. The test consists of 240 questions, so allow up to one hour for completing it in one sitting. You may also complete the test over several sessions by registering free, which will save your responses until you login the next time.

One of the character strengths evaluated on the Character Strengths Inventory is vitality/zest/passion, defined as "approaching life with excitement and energy—feeling alive and activated." This is what psychologists Gretchen Spreitzer and Christine Porath call "thriving with a vital sense of being alive, passionate, and excited."

Your Passion Set Point

But the question remains, how much do passion interventions—even tested interventions—really matter? How much of our capacity for feeling alive and activated, or passionate, is inborn and beyond our control? Is there an internal set point above which we cannot rise?

A set point is defined as an average or mean around which a changing phenomenon tends to vary and to which it tends to eventually return. Examples are body temperature, blood sugar levels, and heart rates, which return to a median state or set point after jogging or exercising. For psychologists, the question is, Does this physical set point phenomenon also apply to the capacity to experience psychological states such as passion and happiness? And if so, does that suggest that no matter what you do to temporarily increase happiness or passion, your efforts will make no real difference in the long run because your upper capacity is set? Is it true that no matter how high you occasionally rise on that scale, you'll eventually return to what is normal for you?

Nutritionists and exercise professionals have known about body weight set points for years—that there is a normal weight for each of us to which we tend to return after temporarily gaining or losing. But these professionals also know that what is considered "normal" for any individual changes over a lifetime. It is far easier to stay slim and at a lower weight in our twenties than in our fifties and sixties, due to changes in metabolism and activity level. Age tends to alter "normal" weight, more often raising it than lowering it.

Earlier research on happiness set points might help shed light on our capacity to experience passion as well. Psychological research has found happiness set points to which we tend to return no matter our temporary spikes and troughs. It is around this personal average that our happiness, satisfaction, and contentment ebb and flow.

The controversy about happiness set points started back in 1978, when a group of Northwestern University psychologists found no significant difference between the long-term happiness of high-stakes lottery winners and a control group who'd won nothing. Perhaps more surprisingly, when these same researchers studied a group of spinal injury patients, they found that the spinal injury group "did not appear nearly as unhappy as might be expected." Both the lottery winners and spinal cord patients spiked in happiness or dipped in sadness after their initial good luck or misfortune, but both groups eventually returned to what had been normal for them prior to winning or being injured.

More recently, psychologist Andrew Oswald undertook a long-term investigation of British lottery winners who had won £1,000 to £120,000. He found that on average, the big lottery winners improved very slightly in measures of happiness and maintained that very slight gain for over a year and a half compared to the small lottery winners and non-winners, both of whose happiness scores remained unchanged. They did find a difference, but that difference was "very slight." On the other hand, in an earlier study, he found that divorcing couples actually rated themselves happier after their divorce was finalized and that they maintained that boost when interviewed two years later. Based on his cumulative results, Oswald concluded that some events at least slightly change us for better or worse and that those changes do not necessarily return to a fixed set point.

Set-Point Marital Satisfaction

Another aspect of the set-point topic as it relates to passion is marital satisfaction. In a fifteen-year longitudinal study of over twelve thousand married couples, psychologists Richard Lucas and Andrew Clark examined happiness associated with positive transitional events throughout marriages—such as one's wedding day, the arrival of children, career or job promotions, and moving to a new house. All of these events boosted people's happiness at the time of their occurrence, but more often than not, people's happiness returned to what was normal for them soon after the event. Nonetheless and importantly, the researchers also found significant differences among individuals. Among their findings were the following:

On average, individuals reacted positively to positive events and then adapted back to baseline levels. However, there were substantial individual differences in this tendency.

Individuals who initially reacted very strongly to a positive event were still far above baseline years later.

Many people exhibited trajectories that were in the opposite direction of that predicted by set-point theory. That is, what might be considered a positive event actually resulted in a lowering of mood.

In general, marital transitions can be associated with long-lasting changes in satisfaction, either positive or negative, depending on the individual.

So which is it? Is marital satisfaction a function of a fixed set point or no set point? The answer turns out to be somewhere in between—at least that's what psychologist Ulrich Schimmack determined in his own long-term study of environmental influences on marital satisfaction. Similar to Lucas and Clark's results, Schimmack found that happiness and couples' satisfaction tended to change in response to significant positive or negative events—such as a promotion, the loss of a job, the birth of a child, or a serious illness—but that overall happiness remained relatively stable over a period of twenty-two years, suggesting the influence of a fixed set point.

Your Piece of the Passion Pie

Does this mean there's a ceiling to how much passion we can experience? Psychologist Sonja Lyubomirsky finally settled the issue in her comparative study of identical versus fraternal twins. Summarizing her results, Lyubomirsky concluded, "About 50 percent of happiness is the result of genetic factors." The identical twins, with the same genetic makeup, were much more alike in happiness as adults than their less genetically matched fraternal twins. That genetic-factor variance accounted for a little more than half the difference. Environmental and other factors accounted for the other half.

Dr. Lyubomirsky's argument for a genetic set point means that no matter what your average happiness level—high or low—it only accounts for half of your happiness or "subjective well-being," as shown in the following chart:

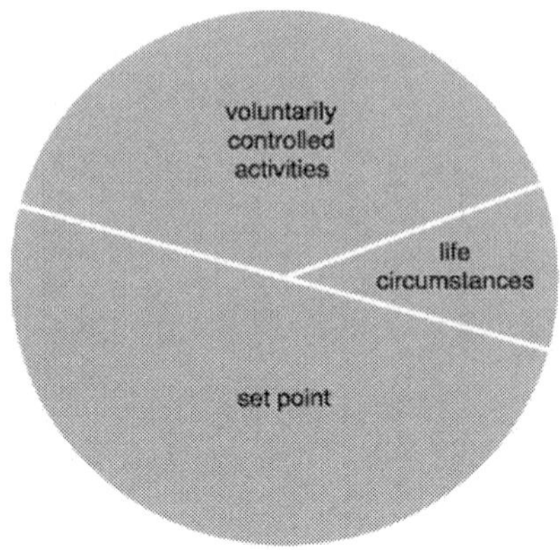

If 50 percent of happiness, satisfaction, and zest is set by genetic factors, as Lyubomirsky's research indicates, she estimates that about ten percent, or the remainder, is the result of "life circumstances." If, for example, you have fewer financial resources than you need, particularly if you fall below the poverty line with several mouths to feed, you are less likely to be happy and content than if you had enough income to feed your family. Psychological research has shown that income makes a huge difference in satisfaction at low income levels but less and less as income rises.

In another area of environmental influence, if you are in a chronically bad marriage or relationship, the daily grind holds your mood below your normal set point, which is one of the reasons that couples are often happier after they separate. To use another example, if you happen to be among a group of friends who are generally upbeat and congenial, that friendship factor tends to raise your set point and keep it raised.

Other than the 50 percent genetic factor and the 10 percent environmental factor from Lyubomirsky's pie chart, we are left with forty percent of happiness determined by what she calls "voluntarily controlled activities." Now we have something we can work with. What are these activities and how are they controlled?

CHAPTER 3

Passionate You!

Margaret Wheatley, author and management consultant, writes that "many of us have created lives that give very little support for experimentation. We believe that answers already exist out there, independent of us. But what if we invested more time and attention in our own experimentation? We could focus our efforts on discovering solutions that work uniquely for us."

This chapter will give you the opportunity to invest time and attention in your own experimentation, focusing on discovering passions that are uniquely yours. You're going to participate in a personal psychological experiment—using yourself as your own subject! The experiment involves what we call the Passion Discovery exercise, in which you'll look to the past, to the present, and then to your possible future for clues to reveal, generate, and deepen your passions.

Webster's Dictionary defines passion as "a compelling emotion or feeling such as love, joy, desire, hope, or a strong sense of attraction or satisfaction." What are your compelling emotions, and where do they come from? The purpose of the Passion Discovery exercise is to help you recall and list as many current, previous, and potential future activities, events, and experiences that have been, currently are, or could be resurrected or developed into fulfilling passions. Once you've listed all of these, you'll look for the underlying connections between or themes of everything you've listed, and then we'll talk about how to prioritize them.

Before you begin this exploration, keep in mind that passion is passion no matter what its source or how others judge it. As Christopher Peterson advises, "We need to be careful not to privilege some passions over others, even though many can be classified as low culture versus high culture. Someone may have a passion for Milwaukee beer over French wine, for Sousa marches over Italian operas, for flapjacks over foie gras, for movies with Adam Sandler over those by Ingmar Bergman, or for novels by Sue Grafton over sonnets by William Shakespeare. In psychological terms, I think these diverse passions function much the same. The bottom line is that we all have activities to which we are drawn."

In other words, each of us is unique and needs not justify or judge his or her passions. Our passions are our own, to be fully lived by us. Or as Janet Attwood, creator of the Passion Test, often says, "You be you!" No one can do Oprah Winfrey like Oprah, nor did anyone do Nelson Mandela like Nelson Mandela. Only you can do you the best.

Guidelines for All the Passion Principle Exercises

Before you begin the Passion Discovery exercise, here are some general guidelines to follow for all the exercises you'll be doing throughout this book:

Use the forms in this book as guides and templates. Each form appears on a separate page at the end of the book. You can copy those, or since you'll be generating far more passion possibilities than the blanks on the form might allow, you can use a notebook or a computerized page devoted to each exercise. That way, your creativity and imagination won't be limited by space.

For each exercise, start by drawing a vertical line down the middle of a blank page (or setting up side-by-side columns on a computer page), then write the name of the exercise at the top of the page and label each column as it appears in the book.

Complete the exercises in the order given and take your time with each, going back to an earlier exercise if you think of something later that you want to add or expand on. It's not necessary to get everything right the first time. After all, it's not about "getting it right." Passion is about continual discovery.

Before you begin, make a commitment to yourself that you will fully engage in each of these exercises and give each your best effort so that you can extract the best that each has to offer. For the first three parts of this exercise, we'll start with instructions, then offer a template for you to use when doing each exercise.

Step #1: Identify Current Passions

Let's start the Passion Discovery exercise by looking at what's happening in your life now.

Instructions: In the left column of your notebook or computer page, list any and all big or small passions that you can think of: those experiences, events, or activities that you love, like, enjoy, and at least occasionally look forward to, even if you aren't sure they truly are passions. List anything that could be the seeds of a passion to explore later. Write as many as you can, as quickly as you can, then think a bit more and list others that come to mind. As you think of additional events, experiences, or passion possibilities over the next day or two, add them to your growing list. For now, leave the right-hand column blank.

Current Passion Experiences or Activities (What I currently like and love to do)	Common Passion Elements (Leave this column blank for the moment.)
1.	
2.	
3.	
4.	

(List as many as you can think of.)	

Here's an example of how one person filled in the sheet. Remember, everyone is unique and different!

Current Passion Experiences or Activities (What I currently like and love to do)	Common Passion Elements (Leave this column blank for the moment.)
1. I love being an uncle.	
2. I like taking 2- to 3-day bike rides.	
3. I love writing for fun and profit.	

4. I love how I feel after meditating.	
(List as many as you can think of.)	

Step #2: Remember Past Likes and Loves That Could Be Passions Again

Let's turn now to the past as a potential source of renewed passions.

Instructions: Think back to events or times in your past—big or small, brief or extended, recent or remote—in which you felt a surge or a slow burn of joy, pleasure, energy, excitement, connection, hope, appreciation, or some other meaningful positive feeling. In the left column of the table below, list each memory or experience as it occurs to you.

Here are some examples. It could be a special office birthday party held last week or a birthday when you were five. It could be a time when you met or spoke to someone you love. It could be a class you took in middle school or a college course. It could be a conversation with a particular person or a series of conversations. It could be something special about your first job or some other job that excited or engaged you. It could be a sunset when you drove home last week, a book you read, or a thought or an idea that struck you while reading a book. It could be a day in an art gallery or standing in front of a particular portrait or landscape. It could be golf, tennis, swimming, or exercising, or it could be going to a movie. It could be any experience or series of experiences about which, at the time, you felt passionate. These memories and events may not be passions now, but they may be seeds that hold the potential for passion again.

Mull over each age and stage of your life in sequence and see what comes to mind. What made you come alive or brought you joy back then? What excited, intrigued, inspired, or delighted you? What did you dream of that you've not yet accomplished? Think of things or experiences you always wished for or wanted and add those to your list.

Write a single word or a phrase that reminds you of the event that brought you joy, satisfaction, or a sense of peace, accomplishment, meaning, or understanding. Try to generate a list of at least fifteen and preferably twenty or more activities, events, and memories. They may occur to you all at once or over the course of several days. As you think of new ones, add them to your expanding list. Again, for the moment, leave the right-hand column blank.

Past Passion Experiences or Activities (What I used to love and like to do)	Common Passion Elements (Leave this column blank for the moment.)
1.	
2.	
3.	
4.	

(List as many as you can think of.)	

Here is how someone began filling this out:

Past Passion Experiences or Activities (What I used to love and like to do)	Common Passion Elements (Leave this column blank for the moment.)
1. I used to love collecting rocks.	
2. I remember being exhilarated after a swim in a lake.	
3. I used to love spending time with small children.	
4. I really liked regularly playing ping-pong with friends.	
(List as many as you can think of.)	

Some people like to leave the past in the past, but fortunately for those of us trying to discover and live our passions, the past can be a rich source of self-knowledge that informs the present. Like Bruce's parents and their lapidary hobby, how many times has each of us felt passionate about an activity for a certain period of time and then simply lost interest in it or never fully developed an interest in it? How many snow skis, pottery wheels, easels, baseball gloves, musical instruments, and golf clubs rest in a closet or in a corner of the attic, never to be picked up again after their initial trial period? The thing is, you never know when an earlier passion might resurface.

When Bruce was in the eighth grade, for example, he saved up enough money to buy a fifteen-gallon fish tank and a few guppies—a newfound passion he picked up from a friend who had such a setup. He couldn't wait for the school bell to ring at 2:30 so he could rush home to see how many babies the females had spawned. It was crucial to get home quickly and transfer the newborns into smaller bowls before their mothers ate them—which seemed to be the predatory nature of guppy mothers.

Much of his meager allowance was consumed by fish food, bowls, and supplies, and he spent a good deal of time at the library researching guppy breeding habits. Both Bruce and his friend considered themselves to be budding marine biologists, a calling that was clearly self-defining at the time. It was all they thought about and all they did. When he wasn't cleaning tanks and feeding fish, Bruce was squatting on a stool with his nose pressed against the glass, fascinated with an ever-changing water world. There was no doubt that he was strongly inclined toward this hobby, which he loved and valued and on which he spent much of his time and limited resources.

The problem was that Bruce's thriving passion quickly over-thrived. As a result of his get-home-quick rescue efforts, the mother guppies were no longer eating their babies and each mother was spawning new mothers who spawned even more until every table and shelf in his bedroom was overwhelmed with bowls of thriving fish. When he finally asked his parents for an advance on his allowance to buy more bowls, his father sat him down and asked, "Son, have you considered Little League?"

After that fatherly conversation, Bruce sold what he could and gave the rest away. Guppies and guppy breeding were suddenly no longer a passion, although years later, he became fascinated with saltwater tanks and now thinks aquariums could again be a passion (the possibility of raising and breeding fish has always been sitting dormant in the back of his mind).

Another source of passions to consider in this Passion Discovery exercise is one's past history of those activities that once were passions and could be again, perhaps in a different form. Randy recalls a story of something that excited and intrigued him as a boy and decades later finally became expressed in his life as a passion fulfilled:

When I was a boy of thirteen, my family spent a summer in the home of a sculptor who was away traveling. I remember walking from room to room and taking in these fantastic shapes and textures the artist had created out of natural wood and stone. They were very sensuous forms that surprised and delighted me with their energy and aliveness—nothing I could really talk about, just feel. I remember saying to myself then, "I want to do that!' I was inspired and wanted to create free-flowing forms of that kind, which put me in awe and wonder.

Decades later, I'd been living in a home that I had completely remodeled when an artist and woodworker friend who had worked on my home came by. He was looking at the ugly bomb-shaped propane gas tank sitting in the front yard and said to me that he had envisioned creating something that would cover these tanks and make them look like beautiful natural rocks. Before I could even think about his idea, I blurted out, "Let's do it!"

Not long after, we created what looked exactly like a big beautiful natural granite boulder; when the propane gas delivery guy came, he asked where the tank had gone! My friend and I started a successful business making rocks and using real ones to create landscapes and water features. At some point, I realized I had become that sculptor the thirteen-year-old boy had dreamt of being!

Step #3: Imagine Future Passions

In Step 1, you listed current passions or events that could be passions. In Step 2, you listed memories of past events, situations, or activities that were passions or might lead to becoming passions. In this step, you'll be using your imagination and your understanding of yourself to look to the future for leads to possible passions.

Instructions: Think of as many activities, events, adventures, and experiences that you might find engaging, uplifting, fulfilling, or meaningful, or that you think you might feel passionate about if you had the time and the resources to engage in them. Once again, leave the right-hand column blank for now. Be creative.

List as many as you can, no matter how wild or outlandish they may seem at the moment; for example, "I would like to fly like Superman, paint like Picasso, write poetry like Elizabeth Barrett Browning, or make love like (fill in the blank)." Don't hesitate or limit yourself, because there may be a way to creatively consider and develop part of them at some point. As Janet and Chris say in The Passion Test book, your only job here is to get clear about the what—simply describe what you would like. You may not know how—and you don't need to yet—so for now just stay with the what.

Potential Passion Experiences or Activities (What I think I might love and like to do in the future)	Common Passion Elements (Leave this column blank for the moment.)
1.	
2.	
3.	
4.	
(List as many as you can think of	

One person started with these ideas. Again, everyone is different.

Potential Passion Experiences or Activities (What I think I might love and like to do in the future)	Common Passion Elements (Leave this column blank for the moment.)
1. I think I'd love playing an instrument and being in a band.	
2. I think I'd like to become a parent.	
3. I think I'd like to plan and take more vacations.	
4. I think I'd like to learn more about financial planning and freedom.	
(List as many as you can think of.)	

When you've finished with Steps 1 through 3—present, past, and future—look over each list again and add any new thoughts, ideas, events, memories, or activities that occur to you. The more you have to work with, the better. This is the raw material from which you will uncover, enrich, develop, and implement more passion. You may be "sculpting" a whole new life of passion!

Step #4: Discover Your Deep Passion Elements

You'll now look for something different: the underlying connections, ingredients, patterns, components, or themes underlying your passions. We'll call these your passion elements, which form the unique basis of passions for you. As in the periodic table of elements in chemistry, these are the most basic units from which you create your best passionate chemistry.

In a sense, you'll be looking at who you are and what strong desires naturally led to your passions—past, present, and future. You'll be looking for those elements that go to the very heart of who you are. These underlying elements can help guide you to developing more passions now or in the future—and not necessarily in the same ways they have in the past.

Instructions: Glance down the left-hand columns of all three lists from Steps 1 through 3. For each event, memory, activity, or experience you listed, consider what it was about it that made it memorable, profound, enjoyable, or satisfying. What are the common elements buried within that particular event or activity that, for you, made it stand out? Was it something about teamwork? Did it have something to do with the outdoors? Was it related to travel, adventure, nature, or education? Was there a sense of belonging, acknowledgement, accomplishment, or competition embedded in that event or memory? What basic elements are embedded there?

For example, we shared that Bruce regularly soaks in his hot tub under the stars at night. For him, that wonder and contact with the sky and stars is an underlying part of what really feeds his passion for close contact with nature, an important passion element for Bruce.

If more than one element occurs to you for each item, write more than one in the right-hand column. You are looking for connections and patterns—elements that occur more than once or several times as you look again at those experiences or activities that gave you pleasure. If "playing soccer" is on your past memory list, for example, you might find and write the elements "teamwork," "challenge," or "competition" next to that activity. You might write all three of them—however many underlying components or elements you think that activity contains.

Do the same with each item on all three lists. Write the underlying component or element in the right-hand column next to each event, activity, or memory. If you need help thinking of elements and connections, consider the following list. Did the event or memory have something to do with the following? Write Yes or No in the blanks:

____ Relationships in general or a particular relationship
_____ Involvement in a group or team setting
_____ An achievement or an accomplishment
_____ Recognition by others
_____ Some sort of quiet satisfaction
_____ Involvement in nature
_____ An insight
_____ A spiritual understanding or connection
_____ More reading
_____ Learning or studying
_____ A physical activity
_____ A personal challenge
_____ A competition
_____ Time alone to relax or reflect

_____ Generating and exploring a new idea
_____ Change and variety
_____ Creating art and beauty
_____ Travel
_____ Animals or pets
_____ Exercising command, influence, or leadership
_____ Beautiful surroundings
_____ Working with children, seniors, or a certain category of people
_____ Giving to or helping others
_____ A greater sense of personal control
_____ Spiritual growth or development
_____ More patience on your part
_____ A quiet, calm environment
_____ Other
_____ Other

Take your time with this part of the exercise. If you can't immediately think of a word or a phrase that describes a passion element, move down the list to the next item in the left-hand column and see what comes to mind. Go back later to fill in any blanks as connections or additions occur to you. If you think of other interests, activities, or potential passions, add them to the bottom of one of the left-hand columns and write the underlying element in the right-hand column next to it. Your past-memory passion list from Step 2, for example, should begin to look something like what follows.

Past Memories or Experiences	Common Passion Elements
1. Playing with other children in the backyard as a kid	Outdoors, friendship
2. Listening to music and dancing in my room	Music, dance
3. Walking alone along the beach in the winter	Outdoors, nature, solitude
4. Watching a bird's nest out my window	Nature, animals
5. Taking vacations in the mountains with my family	Nature, family, outdoors, adventure
6. Being a Boy Scout or Girl Scout	Outdoors, friendship, teamwork
7. Participating in the community food drive	Teamwork, helping others
8. Learning wilderness skills, camping out	Outdoors, accomplishment, nature, adventure
9. Trying out for the sailing team—and making it!	Competition, accomplishment, challenge, teamwork, nature
10. Helping my grandmother bake pies during the holidays	Accomplishment, teamwork, helping others

After finding and listing all the elements you can think of, glance down the right-hand column again and highlight or circle all the elements that repeat themselves. For example, do several memories or activities have something to do with helping others? If so, highlight or circle the words "helping others" every time they appear. Now review the list of memories or events on the left for activities that contain an element of "helping," and if you didn't add "helping others" as an element on your first pass, write it in next to that event or memory now.

Circle or highlight "teamwork" if it appears next to other events or memories. If one or more events, activities, or memories involve reading, circle or highlight "reading" or write "reading" on the right and highlight it. If several items in the left-hand column have something to do with being outdoors, circle or highlight "outdoors" or write "outdoors" and circle or highlight it. Do the same for all items on all three lists.

In the sample past memories/experiences list above, an individual might highlight or circle "outdoors" across from her first memory, "Playing in the backyard as a kid." She might then circle or highlight the "outdoors" element across from memory 6: "Being a Boy Scout or Girl Scout." After highlighting or circling "outdoors," it might occur to her that both of those involve an additional element of friendship, and she might then write or highlight "friendship" in the right-hand column next to items 1 and 6. Her Common Passion Elements column would then start to look something like this:

Past Memories or Experiences	Common Passion Elements
1. Playing with other children in the backyard as a kid	outdoors, FRIENDSHIP
2. Listing to music and dancing in my room	music, dance
3. Walking alone along the beach in the winter	outdoors, NATURE, solitude
4. Watching a bird's nest out widow	NATURE, animals
5. Taking vacations in the mountains with my family	NATURE, family, OUTDOORS, adventure
6. Being a Boy Scout or Girl Scout	outdoors, FRIENDSHIP, TEAMWORK
7. Participating in the community food drive	TEAMWORK, HELPING OTHERS
8. Learning wilderness skills, camping out	outdoors, accomplishment, NATURE, adventure
9. Trying out for the sailing team—and making it!	competition, accomplishment, challenge, TEAMWORK, NATURE
10. Helping my grandmother bake pies during the holidays	accomplishment, TEAMWORK, HELPING OTHERS

Look for patterns. Try to uncover as many possible common elements as you can. If you truly can't find a common element for a particular item, leave the column next to that item blank. It may truly be unique.

Remember that at this point, you're not looking for more specific events or activities (such as those you listed in the left-hand column) but rather the underlying passion elements, such as relationships, intimacy, outdoors, etc. When you are reasonably satisfied with the discovery of your passion elements, look over all the elements that you've circled or highlighted and make a list of those that appear most often or that seem to hold the most promise for deepening, inspiring, or renewing passions.

After you've looked for patterns in the Past Memories list, look for the patterns in your Current and Future Potential lists and then make a list of the elements that most frequently appear in all three lists and give them a number according to how many times they show up.

In the example I've just shared from the Past Memories list, the most common elements are:

Outdoors: 5 entries
Nature: 5 entries
Teamwork: 4 entries
Helping Others: 2 entries
Friendship: 2 entries

When you further develop the passions that have these elements in them, you'll be fulfilling your deepest desires and expressing who you are at the deepest level. You are now ready to create a list of the most meaningful passions for you.

Step #5: How You See Yourself

Thinking about where you are in life now, what elements from your past you want to bring forward, what elements from your current passion list you want to keep, and what you imagine to be the elements that you would want to see more fulfilled in your future. On a separate sheet of paper or a computer page, make a list of what you'd love to see more of in your life that would express the components or elements that are most important to you. These are not necessarily specific action steps at this point, but rather general areas of activity you think you would like to bring into your life. Write a short, simple, snappy, exciting statement that captures the essence of each possibility you imagine. Make these "I see myself" statements, as though you can already see yourself there and doing, being, or having what you want—even though, again, you don't yet know the how.

Vividly visualize yourself being there in the actual experience. Research shows that visualization is a highly motivating step in creating that visualized reality. For example:

I see myself in constant contact with plants and animals I enjoy. (Nature, Outdoors)

I see myself spending fun playtime with my best friends. (Friendship)

I see myself volunteering at my local senior center. (Helping others)

I see myself enjoying loving relationships with my kids. (Family)

I see myself working for a common cause in community. (Teamwork)

I see myself playing on a high-performance sports team. (Teamwork, Competition)

I see myself in deep, meaningful discussions with my friends. (Friendship)

I see myself in constant contact with beautiful landscapes. (Nature, Outdoors)

When you are done making your list, you are ready to prioritize which passion elements are most important to you now.

Step #6: Setting Priorities

In the workshop that Randy and his wife, Dr. Karin Lubin, call Passions and Priorities, people begin to discover that when they get clear about their passions and set them as priorities, their motivation surges and their life takes off. Prioritization is critical to that soaring journey; failure to establish priorities is a quagmire that keeps people floundering in their efforts to live more of their passions.

If you've read Chris Attwood and Janet Attwood's The Passion Test and taken their Passion Test (best done with one of the many trained facilitators now available in fifty countries), you already have a list of your top five passion priorities. If you have not taken the Passion Test but have thoughtfully considered and completed the Passion Discovery exercise steps in this chapter, you now have a list of your potential passions and the common elements they share. Either way, you are now ready to prioritize your list of top passion elements before moving on to creating a Passion Action Plan that will lead to more energy, excitement, involvement, and meaning. With the work you've done so far, you will be naturally led in that direction and your efforts will begin to provide the basis for big changes in your life. Congratulations!

Now take the passion elements you've generated (e.g., friendship, nature) and rank them based on how many times they showed up in the right-hand column of your Past, Present, and Future experiences and activities lists. Then circle the top five elements, meaning the five elements that showed up the most frequently. That will leave you with a list that looks something like this.

1. Friendship: 10 times
2. Nature: 8 times
3. Spirituality: 8 times
4. Teamwork: 7 times
5. Artistic Expression: 6 times

Hold on to this list. You're now ready to put passion into action.

CHAPTER 4

Passion in Action

Sometimes the biggest challenge in life is not deciding what to do—it's deciding what not to do. Your list of potential passions probably encompasses more possibilities than you could explore in one lifetime. So it comes down to a question of where to begin and what to do first—what's best for you, given your priorities, your energy, and your assets.

Now it's time to closely examine how each element that you identified in the previous chapter can deepen and increase passion in your life in both new and old ways. In this chapter, you'll be guided through a list of questions that will lead you, step by step, to a passion-inspired action plan that is aligned with your personal passion elements. You will then be asked to commit to that plan and take the first few steps toward one or more of your identified passions.

Your Personal Passion Action Plan

To begin, make several copies of the Passion Action Plan worksheet below. For each of your personal passion elements, you will be asked to complete a separate Passion Action Plan worksheet. This structure will help you to develop a step-by-step plan for each of your top five passion elements. Begin with the element that showed up most often on your elements list, followed by the next most common element, and so on (e.g., Friendship: 10 times; Nature: 8 times; etc.).

Instructions: You can explore your top three elements or all of them, if you like. To explore each element one at a time, write the name of that element at the top of a worksheet and then thoughtfully answer each of the questions on the form.

PASSION ELEMENT (Name or brief description)

(Examples: "Exercise" and "Love to be around and care for children")

Times or ways this has happened for me in the past: (Original memory, current specific activity, and/or future potential here) - - - - - - -
Ways or conditions under which this or something like this could happen again for me now or in the future:

What I could do to more often find or create these conditions:

-
-
-
-
-
-

What, either within or outside me, would stop me from creating these conditions:

-
-
-
-
-

Would I really like to engage in this or something like it more often? (Circle one.)

Yes No

In what new or old ways might I engage with this passion element again?

-
-
-
-
-

What small step or steps can I take to gain information or further engage my passion potential in this area? - - - -
Will I make the personal commitment to take one of these small steps? (Circle one.) YES NO
If "Yes," when, where, and how will I take this step?

Congratulate yourself when you've completed at least one Passion Action Plan sheet for each of the passion elements you've identified (at least your top three). Together, these sheets or notes make up your first Passion Action Plan. This means you have completed one of the most important steps in the Passion Discovery process by beginning to make your top passion elements actionable—or in other words, real.

If you are still feeling a bit stuck coming up with ideas for activities or actions that could help you focus on the passion elements that make up your most passionate life, use the following list and exercise to help get more concrete.

An Exercise to Trigger More Action Steps

After all the work you've done, you may already have more potential passion activities than you could possibly act on, at least right away. If not or if you still want more, the brainstorming exercise that follows will help you add more possibilities to your list.

Brainstorming research has demonstrated that the best method for generating the largest number of creative possibilities is to start without the help of guidelines. Once your own creativity is exhausted, then use a guide like the one below to generate even more ideas that you may not have thought of on your own.

Instructions: Quickly glance down the list of activities that follows, circling any you currently enjoy or engage in. Add others that you think you could potentially develop, extend, or deepen. Circle or add as many as you think hold promise. The idea is to find as many as possible without thinking you have to engage in any or all of them. When you've finished, look back over your circled or added items and draw a square around those that you think hold the greatest potential for living your passions. Then look back over your squared items. If you see one or more that you would like to seriously consider and further investigate, list those items on a new Passion Action Plan worksheet and answer the worksheet questions to see where your answers might lead.

Passion Action Idea Brainstorm List

Attending a lecture
Attending a live sporting event
Attending or joining a place of worship
Being around animals
Being outdoors
Being part of a group that works on state, national, or international problems
Belonging to a book club
Belonging to a self-help group
Belonging to a social club
Birdwatching
Blogging, instant messaging, or text messaging
Boating or canoeing
Bowling
Browsing bookstores
Browsing through a museum
Buying gifts
CampingCollecting stamps, coins, or other collectables
Cooking or bakingCroquetCycling
Dancing
Discovering a garage sale, auction, or antique sale
Doing crossword puzzles
Doing excercise you enjoy
Doing jigsaw puzzles
Doing photography
Donating time or money to a cause you believe in
Drawing or painting
Eating a great meal at home
Eating a great meal out
Engaging in astronomy/stargazing

Exploring the Internet
Fishing
Gambling
Gardening
Getting a massage
Getting together with neighbors
Giving a massage
Going on new adventures
Going out to a movie, play, or show
Helping others
Hiking
Home decorating and rearranging
Home-improvement or repair projects
Hunting
Immersing yourself in nature or natural settings
Jogging
Joining a hobby group
Joining a singing or acting group
Keeping a journal
Learning a new language
Learning something new
Listening to music
Making up a pleasant daydream or fantasy
Meditating
Needlework, sewing, or knitting People watching
Planning adventures
Planning a day trip or vacation
Planning a meeting or a party
Playing badminton
Playing baseball
Playing basketball
Playing card games or board games

Playing (or working) with children
Playing football
Playing with grandchildren
Playing golf
Playing horseshoes
Playing a musical instrument
Playing with a pet
Playing ping-pong
Playing racquetball
Playing soccer
Playing tennis
Playing volleyball
Reading a favorite magazine
Reading fiction
Reading a mystery novel
Reading the newspaper
Reading nonfiction
Reading for pleasure
Reading with someone and discussing ideas
Shooting pool
Shopping
Sightseeing in the city
Sightseeing in the country
Singing
Sitting quietly for half an hour
Skating or rollerblading
Snow skiing
Spending time alone in silence
Starting an arts-and-crafts project
Strolling in a park
Strolling through a botanical garden or aquarium
Surfing the web

Swimming
Taking a class in a subject of interest
Taking a day trip or a vacation

CHAPTER 5

Passion Factors

After Alice tumbled down the rabbit hole, scrambled to her feet, and dusted herself off in Wonderland, she stumbled across a Cheshire Cat sitting on the limb of a tree and asked the cat which way she should go from here.

"Where is it you wish to go?" the cat asked.

"I'm not quite sure," Alice said.

"Then that should be easy to find," said the cat.

The first step in getting anywhere is knowing where it is you want to go. The first step in increasing and deepening passion is knowing which passions you want to expand and where and how far you want to take them. By now, you've already discovered and listed a full array of intriguing possibilities and directions. In making your choices about which passions to put your attention on now, there can be several factors to consider. We'll discuss these factors in this chapter.

At the end of the last chapter, after completing the exercises, you ended up with three or more completed Passion Action Plan worksheets detailing your plans for taking your first action steps. At this point, to further home in on your most productive choices, you're going to test each action step against four important factors: time, expense, effect on others, and balance.

Lay your completed worksheets side-by-side on the floor or on a desk or table and then compare and rate each action step as you read and consider the factors in this chapter.

As you consider each action step, give it rating it from 1 to 5 and write the rating next to the possible action step on your Passion Action Plan worksheet. The rating numbers correlate with the following conditions:

1 = There is no foreseeable problem with this factor.
2 = There is a potential slight problem.
3 = There is a possible moderate problem.
4 = There are more than moderate issues.
5 = There could be a serious difficulty in this area.

Let's look at each factor in detail.

The Time Factor

The amount of time involved is one consideration when choosing a new passion or expanding or deepening an old one. For example, in one Passion Discovery workshop, a participant said he wasn't surprised that playing golf floated to the top of his potential passion activity list. He said he had always enjoyed watching the game on TV and that he was particularly drawn to the beauty of the greens and the peacefulness of the game. "I think I could learn it all right," he said. "But then you have to practice and play a lot to get any good. I'm just not sure I have that kind of time right now. Work is pretty hectic and we have a baby on the way. I know I'll want to spend most of my free time at home."

He also considered tennis. He said he had played as an adolescent and thought he could pick it up again without devoting nearly as much time to it as golf, and he'd said that tennis would give him more aerobic exercise.

After discussing options with his wife, he decided to

forgo both golf and tennis and instead take up jogging, a passion he had had in college but had let fall by the wayside after graduation. "After the baby comes along," he told the other members of the Passion Discovery workshop, "my wife says she might want to join me to get back in shape again. We can buy one of those three-wheeled baby carriages and exercise as a family. It won't take time away and we can be even closer."

To determine how important time is as a factor, roughly estimate the time commitment for each potential passion activity—low, moderate, or high—and then determine how that time commitment fits with other needs and desires. If you have a general idea of how much time is required, you'll be better able to schedule it. And just like the participant going through this brainstorming and decision-making process, don't stop yourself from enjoying a passion for physical activity or play just because one of them doesn't work for you or fit in your schedule. Keep going until you find one that does! That's why being clear about your most important passion elements is so important. Once you know that there are multiple ways to express that passion element, you have more freedom to live that passion.

The Expense Factor

Unless you happen to be Bill Gates or Warren Buffet and aren't bound by such mundane considerations as money, expense will often be one of the first factors you begin thinking about in relation to living your passions and taking action on them. For some, the idea of devoting any amount of money to pursuing a passion is a nonstarter—but it doesn't need to be.

A love of first-class world travel, including

accommodations at the finest five-star hotels, demands a higher outlay than expanding your teacup collection (depending, of course, on the antique value of your teacups). One former high school stamp collector who signed up for a Passion Discovery workshop said he wasn't sure he could get back into collecting in any serious way without spending more money than he cared to. The small collection he had accumulated in his high school years had long since been given away by his mother, who thought he no longer wanted them. After he discussed the expense factor with the rest of the class, a fellow collector suggested that he keep an eye out on craigslist for "abandoned collections" that often appear at reasonable prices. He liked the idea and thought that might get him started in a way he could afford. This is a fine example of how expense need not be a nonstarter, once you get clear about your passions and share them with others!

As they say in the Passion Test, "When you are clear, what you want will show up in your life, and only to the extent you are clear."

A plastic model-car collection is a lot cheaper than a six-car garage lined with Ferraris or Maseratis. Model-car racing and simulated online racing are both less expensive than shifting gears around an Indi track. A fine cooking class at a local community college is considerably easier on the credit card than a three-month class at the Culinary Institute of America. Big dreams can start simple. You can often take that first step toward living your passions without breaking the bank, while staying open to more abundance than you had imagined, showing up in ways you had not imagined.

The Effect-on-Others Factor

One decision factor for the man who initially considered golf or tennis but ended up selecting jogging was the fact that he could include his wife and his new child in a way that could bring them closer, thereby combining two passion elements for the time and price of one: his passion for enjoyable physical activity and his passion for being close and connected with family. Sharing these passion elements with his wife and child can strengthen understanding, intimacy, and harmony in their relationships.

Two close friends of Bruce—married psychologists in a joint practice—routinely schedule "no-patient" Wednesday afternoons from May through October. They learned to play golf together when they met and continue to play once a week during the season. Wednesday afternoon is their time. They smile as they walk out the door and lock it behind them.

At the other end of the "together/not-together" extreme, golf widows or widowers are not always happy about losing their partner to the game and are sometimes jealous that their partner seems to have more passion for golf than for them—often spending more weekend time on the links than at home. The same holds for a passionate wilderness camper whose partner loves the luxury of their home—an example of a love for warm and cozy that doesn't mix with a passion for rough and rugged.

So the question is, what impact might a new or renewed passion have on someone you care about, and how much do you care about the impact? The implications might be worth discussing with your partner beforehand. Is it an activity that he or she could share or support? How might it benefit or hurt the relationship? A new or expanded passion can present an opportunity to join dreams, hopes, desires, and passions, or an opportunity to support each other's different passions.

John sought advice from an online advice website. He wrote, "My girlfriend and I have been dating for nearly eight months now. We had a rough start, but we have been getting along well the last three or four months. I know she has different interests than I do, and I wonder how that will affect our relationship. I want to travel and live in a warm climate where I can scuba dive and skin-dive. I want to enjoy crazy adventures like sky diving, rock climbing, and backpacking through Europe. She doesn't like to travel much and doesn't want the same adventures that I want. She likes to vacation and just sit inside and read. I love her very much and would do anything for her, but I don't want this to be a problem in the future. Please help. Any advice will be appreciated."

Charlotte, the advisor, responded, "If you have such different interests, you need to talk about your relationship. My own boyfriend and I have completely different passions, but we use them to grow closer. It could be a way to discover more about each other. You may even find that some of her passions rub off on you and vice versa. I love my boyfriend so much that I'm willing to compromise. I'm willing to do things he wants to do and he is willing to do things I want to do, even if it's something we didn't want to do in the first place. Relationships are about making compromises. If you and your girlfriend are not willing to do that, I'm afraid it's not a match made in heaven. Good luck, though. I hope it works out for you."

Everyone is different to begin with, and everyone grows in slightly different ways and directions at different times in their lives. Sometimes a gulf widens that becomes too far to bridge. The challenge is to build bridges that continue to connect and strengthen your relationship.

Of course, doing these Passion Discovery exercises and/or taking the Passion Test together can create a solid new foundation of passion for both of you, one that encourages each of you to support the other at the deepest levels. A passionate partner, after all, can be quite passionate. More about that in "Part II: Living Your Passions."

Balance Factor

The balance factor has to do with how much of your life energy and attention is occupied by each passion and what impact that has on leading a whole and healthy life.

A passionate golfer, gardener, or painter who is single, with no current significant other, has no one else to consider. There's no need to compromise since there's no one with whom to compromise. But that doesn't negate the need for a balanced life. There are other things in life beside golf or gardening or any other single passion. An avid model railroader who spends night after night and all day Saturday and Sunday in his basement is missing something—at the very least, sunshine and exercise. Some would say he's missing life, but that's an individual judgment. The question here is, does a passion or potential passion take over and consume the rest of life? How much room does it leave for more than itself?

Bruce tells this story about Martin, a fellow graduate student at Stanford who was passionate about his major in Middle Eastern history:

When he wasn't hunched over several stacks of history books in the corner of his dorm room, you could usually find him having taken over an entire table in the library's Eastern history section. His dorm mates accused him of never seeing the light of day, an accusation he denied, countering, "How do you think I get to the library?"

Among the activities the rest of us were passionate about and Martin always missed were Saturday afternoon Cardinals football games, the Tuesday evening mixers where we met students from other disciplines and hopefully a potential date, and heading off to the back-alley pub just off Embarcadero, where we could buy a deviled egg and a beer for a dollar during their happy hour.

That is, we never saw Martin at any of these activities until he met Mandy—and it was suddenly no longer just Martin. It was M&M—Martin and Mandy. Mandy was also a history major, one year behind Martin, but she was a lot more outgoing and with strong passions of her own. Soon after they started dating, we began seeing Martin working out at the gym, swimming laps in the pool with Mandy twice a week, and attending sporting events on the weekends. He still carted around two armloads of history books everywhere he went, but it was his and Mandy's initial shared passion for all things history and his newly found passion for her and her interests that expanded his horizons and provided a more balanced life.

Randy likes to talk to his coaching clients about the concept of "harmonizing one's passions," along with a need for balance. We saw that in the M&M example. When Martin's passions harmonized with Mandy's in certain areas, the issue of life balance was resolved for Martin. Rather than holding competing or antagonizing passions or activities, these two new lovebirds were able to blend and harmonize their passions.

When looking to expand a current passion or when considering a new one, the idea is to increase the quality of life, not diminish it with a myopic focus. We'll talk more about when passion becomes an obsession. For now, keep a balance/harmony checklist in the back of your mind. Ask yourself how this new or expanded passion fits into, impacts, or harmonizes with the following:

Family life
Relationships/social life
Professional life
Health (especially time for exercise)
Relaxation and regeneration
Spiritual life (whatever you consider that to be)

Get Clear About Your Passion Factors

Weigh and consider the following four factors when choosing to act on a passion action step: the time factor, the expense factor, the effect-on-others factor, and the balance/harmony factor. And keep in mind that not all factors are equal. Some are more important than others. If you happen to have a lot of time on your hands, for example, the time factor may not be a central consideration since you have plenty of time. Similarly, the expense factor is more or less important depending on how much you need and have to spend on the activity.

That's the reason for your notes after each factor. Each holds a different weight that may change as your life circumstances change. After you retire, for example, you may have more time but less income. If you've been on your own for some time and just started a new relationship, you may have less time than you used to. It's not just your total score that counts. It's your unique circumstances that go into that score.

The following worksheet will help you get clear about

the potential impact of the four factors on each of your potential passion action steps.

Passion Factors to Consider

(Rate each factor on a scale of 1 to 7)

PASSION ACTION STEP #1: ____________________

Time Factor: This passion would require a great deal of time.

Don't Agree Mostly Agree Strongly Agree

1 2 3 4 5 6 7

Notes on Time Factor:

Expense Factor: This passion would incur a lot of expense.

Don't Agree Mostly Agree Strongly Agree

1 2 3 4 5 6 7

Notes on Expense Factor:

Effect-on-Others Factor: This passion would require great deal of patience on the part of friends and family.

Don't Agree		Mostly Agree			Strongly Agree	
1	2	3	4	5	6	7

Notes on Effect-on-Others Factor:

Balance Factor: Considering other life needs and desires, this passion would take away a lot from other important things.

Don't Agree		Mostly Agree			Strongly Agree	
1	2	3	4	5	6	7

Notes on Balance Factor:

Now, once again, lay out your completed Passion Action Plan worksheets side-by-side, this time to see if considering some of these factors changes your choices around which actions to take first for each of your passion elements. Use any notes you've made on the factor rating scales you've completed.

With all four passion factors rated and evaluated for each of your passion action steps, look over your full action plan again, commit to it, and take those first steps.

PART II: Living Your Passions

"Knowing the truth is fairly useless; feeling it is profound; living it makes all the difference."

David Deida

CHAPTER 6

Overcoming Obstacles

Those who are successful at achieving greater passion are often asked about obstacles they had to overcome along the way.

Kelly Clarkson is a great example of someone who faced many obstacles before achieving success. When Kelly's parents divorced, her mother struggled emotionally and financially and Kelly retreated into herself. She dreamt of a career in marine biology until she saw the movie Jaws and was scared out of her wits and out of the water.

She was at a loss for something new to dream about when her middle-school teacher heard her singing in the hallway one day and encouraged her to audition for the school choir. Her passion for music immediately gave her direction, though that path was not always easy. After graduating high school, she was offered a full scholarship to the University of Texas, but she felt so passionate about music by then that she declined the scholarship so she could work as a waitress in Los Angles and pursue a career in music. "I had already written so much music," she said. "I just wanted to try it on my own."

So she followed a passion that eventually led to her winning American Idol, earning six Grammy nominations, and winning two of the prestigious awards. So it's unlikely that Kelly Clarkson will ever have to wait tables again!

Simon Cowell, the TV mogul and former controversial American Idol judge, began his professional life working as a runner on a Stanley Kubrick movie set—when he was able to get along with his colleagues and bosses, which wasn't often. His father, an EMI Music executive (EMI is a British multinational music company headquartered in London and the fourth-largest family of record labels in the recording industry), twisted a few arms to get his son a job in the EMI mailroom. In that low-rung job, Cowell discovered he had a passion for spotting and developing talent, and it ended up catapulting him into becoming one of the most successful talent producers, entrepreneurs, and television personalities in history.

Cowell says he felt especially passionate about developing talent in England before bringing his shows to America. "My proudest achievement," he says, "has been the success of the shows and artists I have been involved with because they were made in Britain." It's passion, he says, that got him out of the mailroom and continues to drive him today.

Passions don't often lead to the celebrity status success enjoyed by Kelly Clarkson and Simon Cowell, but success by most measures is most often preceded and driven by passion, a passion burning hot enough to conquer obstacles. Katie Couric, a network television star, said, "Fame is not what drives famous people. What fuels them is feeling passion about something, then focusing on it and being good at it."

When you discover, get clear about, and act on your passion, you're better able to overcome struggles, disappointments, and discouragement of all kinds. For the person committed to his passion, obstacles simply become the next challenge to overcome, not a game stopper.

In this chapter, we'll explore common obstacles to fulfilling dreams—and how to overcome them.

Help! I'm Stuck!

Let's assume that you've completed the Passion Discovery exercises and that on your worksheets, you've identified some passions and elements you want more of in your life. Let's also assume that you've brainstormed, done a little research, and determined the first steps you'll need to take to get started. Now the question is, how do you motivate yourself to take those steps? That may seem like a foolish question. If you're passionate about something, why wouldn't that passion alone be enough motivation? There are a couple of possible reasons.

1) You still have no solid idea (or at best, you have a very vague idea) of what you want to do.

It's easier to dream a dream than do the day-by-day work to achieve one. Most of us are not like moviemakers George Lucas and Steve Spielberg. Lucas once said, "We always dreamed ahead how a movie was going to be and then just did it." Steven Spielberg, Lucas's competitor and contemporary, added, "I don't dream at night, I dream all day. I dream for a living and then put up it up on the screen."

The difference between dreamers and doers is not that doers don't dream. It's that doers convert their dreams into an action plan and follow it. As Sarah Ban Breathnach writes in her book Simple Abundance: A Daybook of Comfort and Joy, "The world needs dreamers and doers. But above all, it needs dreamers who do." So to follow a dream, you first have to have a dream to follow. Second, you have to convert a dream into a plan with achievable steps. Third, you have to follow that plan, step after step after step.

Go back to your worksheets and review what you've done so far. If it still seems vague, do your research, set your priorities, weigh your options, and consider the benefits and drawbacks. Pick a passion and tweak your first step (if it needs it). If you are one who loves fun, make that first step fun! Then take a deep breath and step out. Pick a reasonable date to begin and stick to that date, always remembering to acknowledge or reward yourself when it's accomplished. Be the visionary with your head in the clouds and your feet on the ground.

2) You feel alone and on your own taking these first steps.

Sometimes it helps to tell a friend or family member about your plan and timetable so they can lend support and ask you about your progress. Bruce's wife Nancy took long walks in the morning, providing herself with exercise and connection with nature, which she thoroughly enjoyed each day until a minor illness forced her to stop for a few weeks. After her physical health improved, she was resistant to getting back to this passion until Bruce suggested she find a walking partner. Once she teamed up with a neighbor, she began walking again, this time having someone both to share the experience with and be accountable to. As a result of taking that step, her original enthusiasm returned—rain or shine.

Feel the Fear and Take the Risk Anyway

Reread what you wrote on your Passion Action Plan worksheets. You may be less vague than you feel at the moment. When we first start out on a new path or in a new direction, it's normal to have many different kinds of feelings. What's behind "vague" or "not feeling solid" for you? If it's just a little fear, that's normal, like stage fright.

Randy says that at the age of fourteen, thinking about giving talks and speeches terrified him. Fear and butterflies churned through his stomach as the time for the speech approached. After a while it occurred to him that time after time, that period of trepidation before a speech actually helped focus his attention and charged him up with energy. He began to accept that the nervousness he felt always preceded a good delivery and presentation. Gradually, he felt quite comfortable onstage and looked forward to presentations. His fear, once he overcame it, was simply part of the learning process.

Anxiety is not necessarily the enemy. Up to a point, anxiety is not all that bad, and there are times when it's actually good. Pursuing a passion—a new one or an old one—often draws you out of your comfort zone. The adventure and the challenge are part of the excitement and part of the fun, as is the anxiety that the unknown and unfamiliar may bring up for you. And that can be helpful. It's moderate anxiety that energizes and sharpens focus.

Consider the passion for rock climbing. Imagine you're high above a sheer rock canyon, with a hundred feet yet to climb and a hundred feet beneath you. Your adrenalin is pumping but not surging. You feel invigorated and fully alive. You're not thinking about problems at the office or back home or what you might be doing this afternoon or tomorrow. You're too focused on your toes and fingertips as you feel for a crevice to inch yourself up another notch. It's only when you suddenly can't find a crevice, when there is none, when sweat starts pouring down your forehead and blinds you, when your knuckles ache and you start to lose your grip—that's when confidence is replaced by panic and anxiety is no longer your friend.

That out-of-control feeling can be seen in what psychologists call an "inverted U anxiety curve," which differentiates helpful anxiety from the not-so-helpful kind. As the shape of the inverted U indicates, performance initially improves as anxiety increases, peaks at an optimal level, then suddenly and rapidly plummets when you feel overwhelmed—when the task suddenly exceeds your perceived ability to cope. Anxiety increases as the unknown increases, but at least initially, so do focus, excitement, and adventure. The known is always the safest, but it's also the dullest and most boring, which is one of the reasons extreme athletes relish activities that take them to the controlled edge of anxiety without crossing over into freefall. Jumping out of bed in the morning is not quite the same as bungee jumping off a railroad bridge. The thrill isn't the same. Neither is the adrenalin or the anxiety.

For most of us, the optimal level of anxiety rests somewhere in the middle range, between safety and security on the one hand and mild risk and anxiety on the other. Since what's new is always unknown by its very nature, most new passions involve challenge and adventure that may require some risk. The height of an Olympic diving board feels safe or intimidating, depending on your diving experience. All horses, to someone who's never ridden, seem large and somewhat menacing. So does distance to the ground for a first-time skydiver or distance to the surface and air for a novice scuba diver. That doesn't mean you shouldn't consider any of these passions. It means you need to be prepared for a little controlled anxiety when you start and as you up the ante.

As a young undergrad at Stanford, Bruce pursued a passion and love of learning. When he applied, there was the risk that he wouldn't make it—that the competition would be too tough. But he knew he would find safety and security in a study routine. He had an assigned dorm room, a standard meal ticket, and a schedule to follow—a plan that was part of a larger structure. As long as he challenged himself and followed through, he knew the university would take care of him.

In their book The Passion Test, Janet Attwood and Chris Attwood talk about the Universe positively responding when we stay focused and committed. In other words, when you take risks, unknown support or resources appear that you would not have experienced unless you had taken that risk.

At times in our life, the outcome of risk taking is hardly assured. Every time we take a chance—whether asking someone out for a date or applying for a job—we risk rejection. If the outcome we picture doesn't come about and we're wise enough to reflect on how and why that happens, we learn how to do it better the next time—or at least how to avoid losing something we know we really want.

As bestselling author Johanna Edwards advises in her online blog:" The next best thing to winning is losing. At least you were in the race. It's better to legitimately fail (by giving it your best shot) than to never try at all. You'll respect yourself a lot more. It's important to remember that even powerful, successful people fail some of the time. Success is often the result of years of trial and error and behind-the-scenes struggles."

Randy likes to remind his audiences that what we often identify as failure can end up being a perfect stepping-stone that can lead us in the direction of something that works even better. You can probably think of a time in your own life when what seemed liked rejection or failure led you to open another door that worked as well or maybe better.

Be willing to accept small, calculated risks and the

possibility of initial failure as normal when experimenting and trying a new passion. Have a backup plan resting on the shelf, but try that initial action or step anyway. As all professional trapeze artists will tell you, keep your net tied and tight when trying a new trick. You will fall. You know you will fall. But with each failure you come one step closer to dazzling an audience and possibly impressing yourself!

Break the Procrastination Habit

It's far easier to stick with the tried-and-true, what you've grown used to, than to try something new. Inertia or an avoidance habit is one of the insidious forces that can hold you back from achieving your dreams. Having the option of taking one of several defined paths doesn't matter if you consistently avoid taking the one that will lead you to living more passionately.

The Japanese have a saying: "If you know something and don't do it, you don't know it." Procrastination is a way of knowing without knowing. Procrastination occurs when you have a "thinking passion" you never put it into action. How many people do you know who have a book in them? Who says they're going to write a book "someday." They're full of talk and enthusiasm about writing as if it were a passion. The problem is, it's not. It's an idea for a passion that rests and waits until it's applied. It's a potential passion.

What causes procrastination? If someone wants to acquire a new skill or involve herself in an activity she might feel passionate about, what keeps her from just doing it? The most frequent reason is laziness. It takes work to learn a new skill. And that work, in the beginning, isn't always fun. It's far easier to put off work and effort in favor of watching TV or playing an innocuous iPhone game. A sense of passionate exhilaration only comes with the enhancement of skill.

Take playing a guitar for instance. It feels awkward when you start. It hurts your fingers until they harden and until you learn where to place them. But if you stick with it, if you work at it, it gradually becomes easier. Then it becomes fun. Just three chords and you begin to feel the passion in your fingertips.

The procrastinator's motto is "I never do today what I can do tomorrow or the next day." On the other hand, as William James, the father of modern psychology, wrote, "Nothing is so fatiguing as eternally hanging on to an uncompleted task."

So the question becomes: What is more exhausting to you over time, hanging on with dread to an uncompleted task or the work of actually completing what you say is most important to you? Some of Randy's clients taking the Passion Test come to realize that it is more torturous to keep putting off living one's passions than to just get on with doing it. Are you at that tipping point?

Of course we already know that the work of completing an uncompleted task is required before the reward is delivered. But how do we keep ourselves on track to enjoying those rewards? Let's say one of the passions you identified on your potential passions list is learning to play the guitar. Let's say that you've always liked the sound of that instrument and that you once read that George Harrison, one of the Fab Four, liked to refer to himself as a guitar fanatic who enjoyed sitting around "doodling" with his instrument while McCartney and Lennon scribbled and scratched out lyrics. And let's say that this is what you'd like to do—get good enough to carry a guitar around and "doodle" whenever you feel like it. But let's say this idea has been spinning around in your head for more than a few years and is always followed by the thought, "I really am going to do that someday. Just as soon as I get the time."

Or let's even say you've gone so far as to buy a mid-priced instrument, tried strumming a few chords, and then leaned the guitar in a corner to gather dust and stir a tinge of guilt every time you pass it by. The problem with learning the guitar—or learning anything complicated—is that it isn't always pure fun until you reach a certain level of mastery. And even then, the masters who are always pushing themselves to greater heights don't necessarily enjoy every minute of practice either. When you're at the very beginning of the learning curve, it's steep! But as dancer George Balanchine once said, "If you want to fly on stage, you first have to learn to dance."

If you view both flying on stage or playing a tune on a guitar as far more fun than learning to dance or play, there may be a part of your brain that would rather skip the learning part and get right to what you've identified as the fun part. Just take the first step.

The Most Famous Excuse

An accomplice to the procrastination habit is the one excuse that people give when they balk at getting started, taking a risk to do something new or different. It goes like this: "But I don't know HOW!"

Einstein did not know HOW he was going to explain what was later explained by his theory of relativity before he was deeply engaged in creative problem solving. Edison did not know HOW he was going to light that first bulb before he began to experiment with countless numbers of materials. Do you think Oprah Winfrey knew exactly HOW she'd become one of the richest women on earth before she got started in her career? The real purpose of an action plan is not to figure out how everything is going to come about with regard to your passion; it's to keep your attention focused on WHAT you see as most fulfilling, what will be the outcome of all this activity you're engaging in, and how great it will make you feel as you do these things you say you're the most passionate about.

Don't fall into the trap of having to know how to do something before you take action. The truth is we usually just don't know exactly how when we get started. As Janet Attwood likes to say, "We are not general managers of the Universe." We need to let go of the *HOW* and stick with doing our part, attaining laser-like focus on the *WHAT*.

How to Overcome Obstacles

A marathon, or any long-term challenge or adventure, always starts at the starting line. Take a moment to consider how far you've come in your passion quest. You've examined passions from the past and the present, as well as possibilities for the future. You've uncovered common elements that go to the heart of several passions. You've made a tentative selection of one or more passions that you might like to add or deepen, and you've developed an action plan with a few first steps. That first step is your starting line.

Once you determine which passion to begin with and where to start, how do you take a solid stance on the starting block and get moving? Since it may not be fun at the start, and even for a little while after that, how do you motivate yourself to take that first step, then the second, and then keep moving forward until it's fun? How do you overcome procrastination, inertia, fear, excuses, or just plain laziness? There are several methods that can help you skirt around or surmount these obstacles.

Research Your Options Using Multiple Sources

The more knowledge you gain about your options, the more that knowledge can help guide your choices. The more you explore a potential passion—google it, read about it, and discuss it with others—the more an obvious choice floats to the top and shouts, "Here I am." At other times, your research and learning helps define your choices by helping you get clear about what you don't want to do.

Nancy Shenker—president of ONswitch, a marketing firm in Westchester, New York—observes that "Entrepreneurs are often so passionate about their ideas, they can lose objectivity. Rather than taking the time to thoroughly plan and research, they sometimes plow ahead with execution, only to spend valuable dollars on unfocused or untargeted activities." In most situations, you need to move forward, but first you need to do your research and consider your direction.

This can also apply to someone embarking on a new passion. Moving ahead at a steady pace with knowledge in hand may produce a better result for the long term.

Following her own series of personal and professional setbacks, actress Sharon Stone knew that she needed to reset her passion priorities and direction in life. As she described in a 2012 interview with AARP: The Magazine, after quickly rising to the pinnacle of movie stardom, she experienced a string of commercial flops. On top of that, her close friend and acting coach, Roy London, died of AIDS; she had two miscarriages; and she went through a bitter divorce from her second husband, San Francisco newspaper editor Phil Bronstein. She lost custody of their adopted son, lost her father to cancer, and then nearly succumbed to a brain hemorrhage that left her in a coma for days and resulted in the loss of 18 percent of her body mass and a lengthy and painful recovery.

But Stone's father, Joseph Stone, who was living with her at the time of his death, had taught her an early lesson that lay in wait as a potential passion. He was always helping others whenever he could, and she credits him with inspiring her philanthropic instincts.

After her own losses, Stone knew she wanted to do something to help others. But do what? What cause or effort should she support? How could she use her fame and name recognition to make a difference? After consulting with friends and doing some research on her own, where to start was easy. In memory of her acting coach, Roy London, she volunteered as chair of the Foundation for AIDS Research. After successfully raising funds for AIDS research, and by that time feeling even more passionate about helping others, she considered offers from other organizations that sought her help. She spoke with friends again and searched the Internet, then narrowed her options down to what she felt most passionate about and where she thought she could do the most good.

Stone now works for Drop in the Bucket, an organization that distributes basic life necessities to those on the brink of starvation in Uganda and other African nations. She has also created a Facebook page to support veterans returning from Iraq and Afghanistan.

Few of us have or ever will have Sharon Stone's fame, beauty, or financial resources. Yet few of us have suffered quite as much pain and loss. Nonetheless, we can still use Sharon Stone's example of how to bounce back from misfortune to passionately delve into something useful and beneficial. It need not be saving the world or feeding starving children in Africa. It need not be charity work, although many find meaning in helping those less fortunate. Charity work is not all that Sharon Stone feels passionate about, but it is a big part of her life.

If you have children or grandchildren, part of your passion usually involves spending quality time with family. Stone didn't need to do research to know that came naturally. But her other passions for filmmaking and charitable giving did require research and resulted in a career as a top-grossing actress and a philanthropist who has come to mean so much to others.

Visualize Where You Want to Be and How It Feels to Be There

Here's more on why we've included "I see myself" statements on your action plan worksheets and why such statements are so powerful. Humans speak a language of words, but our brains more often think in images. If you imagine yourself sitting on a bench in a park that you know well, you won't use words to describe that park and that bench to yourself in your mind. You'll "see" yourself sitting there. If we asked you to describe the view from that bench, you'd translate your vision into words so that we could visualize it.

If we asked you to tell us how you drive to work every day, you'd tell us in words, but what you'd really be doing is describing a turn-by-turn image as you visualize yourself driving that route. Likewise, when you think about a current or potential passion, you usually visualize yourself engaged in that passion, rather than talking to yourself about it. That propensity to think visually can be harnessed as motivation to start a passion or to keep it going if you get bogged down.

Jim Carrey, struggling as a stand-up comic in the late eighties, says he deliberately visualized himself as a successful movie star years before he landed his first offer to do anything big. He says he went so far as to make his vision concrete by writing himself a check for $10 million for "acting services rendered" and dating the check for Thanksgiving Day, 1995. He kept it in his pocket to remind himself of his vision for the future. By 1995, with that check still in his wallet, he was a top comedic actor earning well over $10 million a picture.

Rosabeth Moss Kanter, a professor at Harvard Business School and author of Confidence: How Winning Streaks and Losing Streaks Begin and End (Kantner 2006), states what psychologists have known and used in therapy for years. She writes, "A vision is not just a picture of what could be. It is an appeal to our better selves, a call to become something more."

Dr. Cathryne Maciolek, a Washington, DC, therapist, regularly uses visualization to motivate her clients. She finds that "directed visualization" often helps clients "picture a goal and reinvigorate themselves toward it" when they get discouraged or down in the dumps and need a motivation jolt.

When working as a therapist, Randy used visualization to help create the images and associated feelings necessary to relax and be receptive to new ways of being and acting. Now as a personal coach, what Randy has found most useful in the Passion Test process is called the "passion marker," a milestone that would let you know you're living your passion fully. It's a concrete piece of evidence that is stated as already having happened, not merely something that could or might happen in the future.

If we continue to view something as being in the future, that is often where it will remain. We need to put ourselves there to be there. Randy says that if your dream or passion is to become a world-renowned concert pianist, picture yourself having just finished a perfectly performed concert at Carnegie Hall to thunderous applause. Sound exaggerated? It happens to be a technique that is most effective in raising inspiration and motivation to begin taking the steps in that direction. This is not the only image or visualization to get you there, but it's completely OK to shoot for the stars in order to get yourself headed for the horizon.

According to Jack Canfield, best-selling author of the Chicken Soup for the Soul series and The Success Principles, passion markers are where the rubber meets the road in beginning to move in the direction of living one's passions.

Of course, if gardening is one of your potential passions, visualization alone won't plant a rosebush or a tomato plant. As most gardeners will testify, while they're thumbing through those winter catalogues or browsing plants online, they visualize what they hope their garden will look like in the spring and summer. During those long winter months, it's their visual imagination that keeps them revved up for that first warm-weather soil turning.

Try a visualization experiment. Think of a passion that you would like to begin living or expanding. Would you like to play the guitar well enough to guitar-doodle like George Harrison, or play in a band, or perform for your friends or your children? Would you like to travel the country or travel the world? Would you like to grow vegetables or flowers in your backyard? Whatever passion you're considering, take a moment and visualize yourself fully engaged in that passion, just as you would like to experience it down the road. See yourself there, completely focused and passionately involved. Hold that vision a few seconds and savor it.

Now ask yourself, how would you feel if you were

actually there, fully engaged? Notice how you feel some of those emotions just by visualizing and strongly imagining the experience. If you're having a difficult time visualizing, one technique for triggering your own imagination is to look at travel or other magazines or coffee table books that have images related to your passion. I've had some of my most inspirational moments in waiting rooms thumbing through magazines I might never have seen otherwise.

Finally, refer to your Passion Action Plan worksheet and review what you identified as your first steps. Visualize yourself taking those steps. If the first step feels too big, visually break it down into smaller steps. Now visualize yourself TAKING that first step. SEE yourself going through the steps until you can visualize yourself participating in your passion. If a step involves gathering the necessary information and tools, see yourself gathering them. If that step requires setting up an appointment to speak with someone, see yourself meeting with that person. If that step requires purchasing something, see yourself making that purchase. Whatever it takes, see yourself taking that action.

Be sure to watch your thoughts as you do. Nothing will sabotage your visualization faster than saying to yourself silently or out loud, "That'll never happen," or "How in the world could that be possible?" and all other self- and passion-negating statements. Instead, you can simply say, "It's done." Even if you don't believe it at first, continue with the visualization and statements of affirmation until you do. Affirmations only work if you're open to your visualizations or even something better coming to pass. When people say that affirmations don't work, it's usually because either consciously or unconsciously, they're holding these negating thoughts, cancelling out their positive intentions for themselves.

Visualizing an imagined result and then taking that first step can charge up your engines and get you started. Eventually, once you're on your way, passion runs on its own steam. You will enter that psychological state of flow we spoke about earlier. And that's a very good place to be.

Review Your Passion Action Plan Worksheets Repeatedly

If you've gotten this far in the book, you have undoubtedly already taken steps toward creating, enlivening, and deepening passion in your life. If you reach that point where once again, too many choices leave you sitting at a fork in the road, eternally looking right and left without ever standing up and walking down either path, it may be time to review again what's most important as well as the underlying elements you began to identify earlier in your Passion Discovery exercises.

If the actions you've taken are not the ones getting you closer to living your passions more fully, it may be that your passions have shifted or perhaps, for example, that the element of Friendship has become more important than that of Creativity at this time in your life. If these elements and their importance to you have not shifted, then perhaps it would be helpful to repeat the prioritization process in the Passion Action Plan introduced in Chapter 4, which helps you formulate new action steps, and then prioritize what to do first. This could be all you need to do to push Restart.

Organizing as a First Step

Bruce shares this instructive story about his early

attempts at organization: More often than not, my father's basement workbench resembled a disaster area—tools scattered everywhere, often covered with multicolored paint blotches he neglected to clean off; nails and all variety of pins and clips haphazardly dropped or tossed in all directions; and layers of sawdust that had blown back from his band saw and settled in every available crack and crevice. My father's constantly evolving tool-and-scrap sculpture regularly frustrated him—but not enough to clean it up. Twice a week or so, the family would hear a string of moans and curses drifting up through the floorboards as his frustration showed itself.

I remember going downstairs and looking at that workbench one afternoon when my dad was at work—and feeling sorry for him. I decided to clean and organize it. I elbowed everything off the surface into three wooden boxes and sorted through the contents, tossing all the bent and rusted nails, odd chunks of wood, and handfuls of assorted unidentifiable objects into a quickly overflowing trash can. Once I started organizing, I just kept going. I brushed, cleared, and scraped off as much of the dust, dirt, grit, and grime as I could, all the way down to bare wood, and then sat the boxes back on the bench. I rummaged through the scattered tools and hung what I could on their pegboard hooks, then emptied two under-bench drawers and lined up the remaining miscellaneous screwdrivers, sanders, and odd gadgets in their places. Then I stood back and admired my work.

My dad never said anything when he arrived home after work that evening and wandered down to the basement, but he did stop cursing and his mood improved for the next few weeks as he was able to get his projects done in record time, producing some of the most beautiful birdhouses as gifts for the neighbors. Then the pile slowly started stacking up again, and his groans and muttering started drifting back up through the floorboards. Actually staying organized was clearly not an activity he had mastered, although his passion for building useful items had clearly benefited from that effort.

Oddly, I thought about cleaning and organizing that workbench years later when I started graduate school at Stanford. Stanford was on the quarter system, which meant four intensive classes every ten-week quarter, each class meeting three times a week and each requiring seemingly endless experiments, papers, and reports, along with memorizing reams of facts from stacks of books and journals. It was a mindboggling task for which you had to be organized and hit the ground running.

I spent many late nights with piles of papers, books, and study cards scattered across a desk that suspiciously started to resemble my dad's workbench—minus the sawdust and rusty nails. The only way to get the job done was to set priorities and organize my time and materials. It was a lot of work, but once I was done, momentum took over and kept me going. The next thing I knew, I had finished a day's work and was ready for a good night's sleep to start in again the next day.

Ever since those Stanford days, whenever I'm having a tough time getting started, I start by organizing. I clear off my workspace and gather my tools and materials and whatever information I need. By the time I do all that, I'm off and running and the initial thrust carries me forward.

Consider Each Step as a Reward

The psychological definition of successive approximation is "the gradual shaping of a behavior by reward that gradually gets one closer and closer to a desired outcome until that outcome is reached." When a realist landscape artist stands in front of a blank canvas and stares out across a landscape with the intention to paint it, the first thing she does is draw a few simple lines across the canvas to indicate the approximate location of the horizon and a few major objects. The artist doesn't care about the details at that point. All she cares about is the big picture. Then, one step at a time, she "shapes" or "successively approximates" what she sees in front of herself, starting with big splotches of shape and color, then working down to detail, and then to very fine detail until what is seen on canvas looks very close to what is in front of her. In each step, the artist begins to see the gradual completion of the work. And in that process, each step becomes its own reward, leading to the next step and its reward and then the next, until completion.

When Michelangelo was asked how he managed to carve David from a block of marble, he allegedly said, "I just kept chipping away, standing back and looking, then chipping again until David appeared." Word by word takes the place of chip by chip when someone writes a novel. And no novelist gets a novel written right the first time he tries. He starts with an idea, expressed in an initial block of words, and then keeps chipping away or adding until the novel in mind appears in print. Like the sculptor, the writer is creating images with words, then sculpting (editing) those words to complete the creation over time. And it may take many iterations or versions before the work is complete or ready for publication.

Consider realization of a potential passion as a series of small steps, each of which gets you closer to what you've visualized. Unless you're working under a very tight deadline, you don't have to get it right the first time or even at all. All you have to do is get a little closer with each step. The more you delve into a passion and the more you develop your skills and learn which steps are most effective, the better you get and begin to realize it's a continuous process—and that in itself becomes the reward. With a true passion, you never arrive. It becomes more about the journey than the destination. Michelangelo learned and experimented his entire life. In that sense, his work was never done. Here are some suggestions to get started:

1) Set Incremental Goals and Objectives

It takes more effort to start a rock rolling than to keep one rolling. Likewise, there's a certain point where critical mass is reached and the reward equals the effort. The activity starts to roll along with less and less effort. When you're learning to play the guitar, to use an example we've used before, the first two chords are the most difficult to learn and the most painful to the ears and fingertips. But once you've mastered a third chord, a wide world of three-chord songs suddenly opens up. The desire to learn the next chord is heightened. And after a bit more fitful fingering, it begins to sound and feel as if the guitar is worth playing. Though much more practice lies ahead, the effort is increasingly easy and the results more pleasing and rewarding.

Most writers write a certain number of pages every day or devote a certain amount of time to writing. Screenwriter John August, in his How I Write Blogs, says he shoots for "five good script pages a day." William Faulkner tried for ten pages a day. Ernest Hemingway, Faulkner's competitor and contemporary, didn't concern himself with numbers of pages. He woke up at 6:30 in the morning and wrote standing up until eleven. Each writer has his or her own method, but what they share in common is setting a daily goal and sticking to it. It's not simply passion and a talent for writing alone that gets a book written—it's passion and talent backed up with commitment and disciplined effort. Many successful people may initially lack the talent but carry the day by giving dogged commitment and attention to what gives their lives the most meaning and satisfaction.

Psychologist Barbara Fredrickson, in her book Positivity (2009), recounts a traditional Cherokee folktale. "One evening an old Cherokee told his grandson about a battle that goes on inside people. He said, 'My son, the battle is between two wolves inside us all. One is Evil. It is anger, envy, jealousy, sorrow, regret, greed, arrogance, self-pity, guilt, resentment, lies, false pride, superiority, and ego. The other is Good. It is joy, peace, love, hope, serenity, humility, kindness, benevolence, empathy, generosity, truth, compassion, and faith.' The grandson thought about it for a minute and then asked his grandfather, 'Which wolf wins?' The old Cherokee simply replied, 'The one you feed.'"

Starting or growing a passion requires regular feeding, effort, and attention. Pick the number of times and/or the amount of time you are willing to feed this passion during the course of a day, week, or month. Then watch the Good Wolf grow.

2) Don't Accept Excuses

We began to discuss this when we addressed procrastination. As the popular personal development guru Wayne Dyer's book title commands, Excuses Be Gone!

Chronic fatigue syndrome largely confines Laura Hillenbrand to her home, where she sometimes sleeps for days, waking up for an hour or two here and there. Rather than allowing this debilitating condition to totally ground her, she travels the world in her imagination by writing books, including the best-selling story of the race horse Seabiscuit. Even if she didn't sell, she would write anyway—slowly, but she would still write. She works her passion around her condition. And she could easily have used her condition as an excuse not to live her passion. The world is glad she didn't.

3) Don't Wait Until Something Is Perfect

In coaching sessions, Randy often hears people cite all the reasons why taking certain actions toward living a passion will not be the "right" ones, or why there are no "right people" to do them with. It can be a fine excuse for not getting started, but not one likely to lead to results, let alone the perfect situation.

Suppose you think that volunteering or helping others is an activity that you believe holds promise as a passion in your life. The underlying element of wanting to be of service may become more important to you at some point. Many organizations, local groups, and international groups can use your help, but in your research you may not yet have identified the one you could feel most passionate about. Don't stop or wait—continue with your research efforts. And in the meantime, find local organizations that are looking for help and pitch in.

Sometimes you simply can't completely know you are passionate about something until you meet the people and try doing the work. Local organizations are often looking for help on a short-term basis, perhaps for just one event, without asking for a commitment of time beyond the immediate requirement. If helping others, the environment, or raising money for a cause could be a passion for you, look locally and short term as a start to finding the perfect cause.

4) Just Do It!

Have you ever seen pictures of how they had to start the first automobiles? The engines had no ignition system like modern vehicles. There was no key to turn or button to push to start an engine purring. You had to hop out of the driver's seat, walk around to the front, bend over, and turn the crank until the engine sputtered and caught. Only then could you jump back behind the wheel, tap your foot on the gas, and head out.

In Ray Bradbury's classic sci-fi novel Fahrenheit 451 (Reprint 2013), one of his characters says, "We'll just start walking today and see the world and the way the world walks around and talks, the way it really looks. I want to see everything now. And while none of it will be me when it goes in, after a while it'll all gather together inside and it'll be me. I've got one finger on it now; that's a beginning."

If you want to start a new passion, visualize yourself already engaged in the world of that passion, then set a daily or weekly goal that moves you closer with each step. With that vision and goal in mind, follow the old Nike shoe-ad slogan: Just do it! Every time you do, you move a step closer to a more passionate life.

CHAPTER 7

Passion versus Obsession

Sometimes what we think might be a passion, others see as an obsession. It's important to know the difference because one is healthy while the other can damage your physical health, your mental and emotional well-being, and your relationships.

The Merriam-Webster Dictionary defines passion as "a strong liking or desire for, or devotion to an activity, object, or concept." That same dictionary defines an obsession as "a persistent disturbing preoccupation with an idea, concept, or activity." The crucial distinction between the definitions for passion and obsession lies in the words "persistent" and "disturbing." Persistence is usually considered a positive trait. "Disturbing" is rarely considered positive, although Merriam-Webster doesn't operationally define what's meant by "disturbing." Disturbing to whom? What is it about a particular activity, object, or concept that would make it disturbing?

Let's look at what the experts have to say about what pushes passion into obsessive realms—and what you can do to return to balance if your passion gets out of hand.

Harmonious versus Obsessive Passion

Psychologist Robert Vallerand has done the bulk of the research on the connection between passion and obsession and where the line between them is. Vallerand differentiates between what he calls "harmonious passion" and "obsessive passion." In a video interview, he described the difference this way: "In harmonious passion, you get nothing out of it beyond the activity itself. You engage it in for the pure love of the activity. You enjoy it, you get lost in it, you have a great time doing it, and afterward, you feel a high level of satisfaction or warm personal pleasure."

An obsessive passion, on the other hand, is one in which "internal pressure forces an individual to engage in the activity." Vallerand goes on to state that "research in a variety of life domains has shown that harmonious passion typically leads to adaptive outcomes while obsessive passion tends toward less adaptive and even maladaptive outcomes."

In one study of those who regularly practice yoga, Vallerand and his research colleagues found that those who were harmoniously passionate about yoga "experienced a significant increase of positive emotions both during and after yoga exercise," while those who were obsessively passionate "experienced negativc emotions before, after, and even while engaged." Those yoga enthusiasts who were harmoniously passionate practiced for many reasons, but their primary motivation was their love of yoga. The obsessively passionate felt that they had to practice yoga, that they had no choice, and that they were driven. They may have derived side benefits from yoga—exercise, for example—but none of those benefits included a love of the activity itself.

There were no observable external differences in the individuals in one group compared to the other, other than the individuals' underlying motivations. The harmoniously passionate and obsessively passionate groups' enjoyment of and satisfaction with yoga was totally different. Both groups got the same stretching and exercise benefits, but the harmonious group found more joy and pleasure in the practice of yoga.

What Role Does Choice Play in Passion?

Vallerand says harmonious passion is "freely chosen for the pleasure of the activity." Harmonious passion is characterized by autonomy, balance, and flexible persistence. Those with obsessive passion, on the other hand, have difficulty disengaging, feel anxious and uncomfortable when not engaged, and are often conflicted between their obsession and other aspects of their life.

In one study of online game players, researchers found that gamers who measured high in harmonious passion experienced significantly stronger positive emotions while playing, while those who scored high on obsessive passion experienced more negative emotions during play, after playing, and when prevented from playing. Many of the obsessives emphasized winning over playing and were "significantly more upset" when they lost.

Every once in a while, someone who doesn't know Bruce well asks whether he is obsessively passionate about writing. It clearly is a passion. He enjoys writing. He spends a lot of time at it. He considers it valuable. He feels it's an important part of who he is. The question is, has he crossed the line? Is his passion for writing harmonious or obsessive? Does it interfere with the rest of his life? Does he experience withdrawal if something stops him from writing? Is it an out-of-control obsession? Is he in denial? Would he be the last to know if he were obsessive?

We'll let you know in a moment, after we share with you a great test you can use to evaluate the issue of harmonious versus obsessive passion. Dr. Vallerand developed and validated a seventeen-item passion/obsession scale to measure the difference between obsessive and harmonious passion. The scale below is similar to Vallerand's and ferrets out the same differences. To avoid test bias, Vallerand's experimental subjects were not initially told the difference between the two. For our purposes, since we've already discussed the difference, we're simply interested in helping you see where you stand on the harmonious/obsession dimension—so be as honest as you can when you rate yourself.

The Harmonious/Obsession Scale

Instructions: Think of an activity that you like or love, that's important to you, that you look forward to, and on which you now or once spent a significant amount of time.

Write the name of that activity here:

While keeping this activity in mind, use the scale below and circle your level of agreement with each item. You'll first answer questions about harmonious passion, then obsessive passion.

Don't Agree Mostly Agree Strongly Agree
1 2 3 4 5 6 7

Harmonious Passion

1. This is something I love to do.
1 2 3 4 5 6 7

2. When I engage in this activity, I tend to lose track of time.

1 2 3 4 5 6 7

3. This activity says a lot about who I am and what I like.

1 2 3 4 5 6 7

4. The more I learn about it and get involved in it, the more I enjoy this activity.

1 2 3 4 5 6 7

5. When I do this, I feel engaged and involved.

1 2 3 4 5 6 7

5. Doing this is part of what I like about myself.

1 2 3 4 5 6 7

TOTAL HARMONIOUS SCORE ☐

0 - 10 = Low
11 - 20 = Moderate
21 - 35 = High

Obsession

1. I get nervous when I don't engage in this activity for a long time.

1 2 3 4 5 6 7

2. When I am doing something else, thoughts of this

activity often distract me.

1 2 3 4 5 6 7

3. Sometimes I feel as if I absolutely must perform or engage in this activity.

1 2 3 4 5 6 7

4. I will do this activity even when I know I should be doing something else.

1 2 3 4 5 6 7

5. This activity sometimes interferes with my social life.

1 2 3 4 5 6 7

6. Friends and family sometimes say I engage in this activity too much.

1 2 3 4 5 6 7

TOTAL OBSESSION SCORE ☐

0 – 10 = Low
11 – 20 = Moderate
21 – 35 = High

How do your total scores compare? Did you rate yourself low, moderate, or high in harmonious passion and obsessive passion? How does this fit with what you'd like to be? Look back at your scores on individual questions on each scale and consider what you might like to modify or change.

Bruce's Scores on Writing

In terms of Bruce's writing, his total score on the Harmonious Passion Scale is 35—as high a score as that scale allows. His total score on the Obsession Scale is 7. On question 2 of the Obsession Scale, he is occasionally distracted by the thought of something he wants to write while he is in the middle of something else, and he sometimes takes time to jot it down so he won't forget it. But that doesn't happen very often, so he gave himself a low score of 2 on question 2.

On obsession question 4, he occasionally writes a bit longer than he should when he has chores to do, so again, he gets a score of 2 on obsession question 4. Finally, on question 5, Bruce's wife occasionally complains that he spends too much time writing, so he scored himself 3 on question 5. That gives him a total Obsession Score of 7, which is in the mid-to-low range for obsession. Not bad if he's being honest with himself. And why shouldn't he be? If he lies to himself, who does he fool?

Rod Stewart's Trains: Harmonious or Obsessive Passion?

Raspy-voiced British singer and top-selling recording artist Rod Stewart has several passions besides singing and performing. He loves architecture and interior design and enjoys leaning back in bed in the evenings and thumbing through the latest architecture and design magazines. He has furnished his palatial Beverly Hills estate with eighteenth-century French and Italian pieces that were featured in Architectural Digest. He is so passionate about collecting art and furniture, he tells Lifestyle magazine, "I would give anything to work at Sotheby's." He is also passionate about rugby and frequently plays with a group of friends when he's in England.

More recently, Stewart has revealed a secret passion for HO model trains—a potential passion of Bruce. Bruce has always enjoyed Rod Stewart's songs, and as an HO model train enthusiast himself, he was delighted to open Model Railroader magazine to a feature spread describing Stewart's massive 23-foot-wide by 124-foot-long HO post–World War II railroad layout of downtown Manhattan, rendered in jaw-dropping detail and containing over a hundred individually crafted structures. Stewart had emailed Model Railroader, informing them, "Having been a model railroader for twenty years and an avid reader of your magazine for longer, I thought you may be interested in publishing some photos of my layout."

The article noted that Stewart built parts for his layout in hotel rooms while on tour. On his sixty-three–city American tour in 2007, he says he commandeered a suite in a major Chicago hotel, returning after each performance to work on one of the model buildings he carried with him in a protected suitcase. "I pity a man who doesn't have a hobby like this one," Stewart told Model Railroader. "It's just the most supreme relaxation. Everyone should have one hobby that really captures their interest."

So the question is, is Stewart's modeling hobby a passion or an obsession? He certainly loves the activity, which meets one of the five criteria for passion. There's no doubt he spends a good deal of time pursuing it. He clearly considers himself a model railroader—the "self-definition" part of the passion criteria. He considers it of enough value to share his passion for it with the rest of us model railroaders. As to whether or not it's an obsession, that depends on the following:

Whether or not he models for a reason other than love of the hobby (He certainly seems to love it.)

Whether it interferes with rest of his life (He still records, shows up for concerts and interviews, and continues to play rugby with his friends.)

Whether it interferes with his relationship with his wife, his children, or his friends (We would have to ask them.)

Obsessive Passion Blocks Itself

You don't undertake an obsessive passion for the love of the activity, and it doesn't simply fill your time. It overfills it and then preys on your mind when you aren't involved. An obsessively passionate person is a computer gamer who spends nearly every free minute playing online, a bodybuilder who spends every evening at the gym and then adds another six or eight hours every Saturday and Sunday, a competitive ballroom dancer who does nothing but dance, or a compulsive reader who spends most available hours with his face buried in a book and then falls asleep with his night-light on and a book flopped open in his lap.

As University of Michigan psychology professor Christopher Peterson writes, "What makes a passion obsessive is that it actually gets in the way of itself. A hobbled jogger is not much of a jogger and will become ever less so as his or her jogging continues. Someone obsessively passionate about gambling will likely run through his or her money and not be able to place future bets."

As blogger John Hagel writes, "When I was a boy, I was obsessed with chemistry. I had a chemistry lab in my home and I couldn't wait to retreat to my little lab and conduct the most amazing experiments, exploring all kinds of permutations of chemical mixtures. When I was not in my lab, I was devouring chemistry textbooks. People said I was passionate about chemistry, but they were wrong—I was obsessed. I was using chemistry as an escape from a very difficult childhood. It was a survival mechanism, not a means to achieve my full potential."

Hagel goes on to say, "We are all familiar with these sorts of cautionary tales of people who are so consumed by their passions that they lose their social standing, meaningful relationships, and ultimately their mind. Their professional and social lives fall apart as obsession grips their every waking hour, crowding everything else out. It's no wonder people fear passion."

Randy also has a passion for writing—thank goodness—or we would not be sharing this marvelous passion project. He has many times observed in himself and others a sudden obsession with an activity that taken by itself would seem harmless. However, when you add the fact that devouring mystery novels, one after another, can keep you from completing that project you say is important to you—writing a book, completing a training or course of study, or working at a job that could lead to solid personal and professional advancement—it becomes clear that such obsessive activity has become a defense mechanism against feeling the fear that may come up around failure or even success in some aspect of life.

How to Unhook from an Obsession

When you take the Harmonious/Obsession Scale test, if you discover that one of your passions has actually moved into the realm of unhealthy obsession, take heart—there are several things you can do to get back to a healthier place. Here are several ideas for you to consider.

1) Thoughtfully Consider Your Priorities

Even as a child, cellist Yo-Yo Ma had a passion for classical music. Music filled his home and filled his life. His mother was a classical singer and his father was a violinist and music professor. Ma began studying the violin and then the viola at the age of three, settled on the cello at the age of four, was performing for audiences by the age of five, and performed for presidents Kennedy and Eisenhower at the age of seven. By his fifteenth birthday, he had graduated from Trinity School in New York and had already appeared as a soloist with the Harvard Radcliffe Orchestra. But before launching his solo career, he decided to take time off to experience life beyond music. He still practiced, but just not for the same long hours. He now calls those off years "an emotional bank account from which you draw on the rest of your life."

Psychologist Scott Kaufman writes in his review of the effects of Ma's decision to take time off, "If those years of undisciplined learning were detrimental to his career, I am hard-pressed to detect it. Yo-Yo Ma is one of the greatest cellists of all time, noted not just for his incredible talent and dedication but also the breadth of his accomplishments, his compassion, thoughtfulness, knowledge, and positive enthusiasm. In other words, his harmonious passion."

Jimmie Johnson—the only driver in the history of NASCAR to win five straight championships—is considered the most influential athlete today by Forbes magazine. In an interview for CBS Sunday Morning, Johnson said racing has been on his mind ever since he can remember and that his parents supported his passion for machines and racing early on. He started with a dirt bike at age four and was racing at five, paying for entry fees by doing chores around the house. Now, at age forty-four, married and with a daughter, he still feels as passionate about racing as he ever has, but he tries to balance his life by spending time with this new passion: raising his daughter.

As Mahatma Gandhi once said, "Action expresses priorities." The reverse is also true. When you understand your passions and priorities, take them seriously, and pay attention to them, action follows. And when you understand the difference between harmonious passion and obsessive passion, you can better choose your actions to fit your priorities.

Randy reminds us that the number-one tool he uses in his coaching practice when he begins working with a client is the Passion Test process. He does this because the Passion Test forces people to prioritize those things they say they love the most, make them feel the best, and are most important to them. It often helps people sort out what they truly love from their obsessions. And the exercises we provide in this book will serve in the same way when you look at those deeper elements and how they're served by your passions.

2) Look to the "Inside" for Motivation

Obsessions are more than done—they're overdone. One woman Bruce treated in therapy said she was passionate about bicycling. She owned a high-end racing bike, belonged to a riding club, and rode with the best of them two hundred miles every weekend. Beyond that, she rose at 4:30 every morning on weekdays, rode fifty miles—usually in the dark—before showering and going to work, and then rode a shorter twenty miles in the evenings. When it snowed in the winter and she couldn't go out, she rode a stationary bike in her living room.

Instead of resting and healing when she was injured, she "biked through" her injuries. She had no other life—there was no time for one. Cycling squeezed everything else out.

Most cyclists aren't that obsessed with cycling, but again, the question is, where is the line between passion and obsession and when is it crossed? When Bruce's biking client finally figured out the "why" of her obsession, she was able to admit that shutting out everything else protected her from having to figure out what that everything else was, from examining what was and was not working in her life.

The crucial questions for those engaged in obsessive passions are (1) What is the obsession protecting you from? and (2) What are you avoiding and why are you avoiding it?

3) Keep Track of Your Time

A major test of an obsession is the amount of time spent engaged in its pursuit. Obviously, for our obsessed biker, cycling, working, and sleeping occupied 80 percent of her time. Some activities do take time. The question is one of choice. Obsessions set their own schedule and run on their own steam. Harmonious passions, on the other hand, are less a compulsion and more a desire. They are neither forced nor driven. They allow a choice, and there's no inner price to pay for making that choice. They allow you to do other things with your time without any longing and without withdrawal. But our biker was unable to stop her daily cycling. Whenever she did, she sank into a depression. So that made her passion an obsession.

Like any obsession, there are two primary methods of regaining control—cold turkey and tapering off. Tapering off is usually the easiest, although both are easier if you can figure out—or seek help figuring out—the reason for the obsession, the "why" of it. If you think your passion is an obsession, ask yourself these questions about it:

> What thing are you avoiding when you engage in your obsession?
> What feelings are you avoiding feeling when you engage in your obsession?
> What is the obsession replacing?
> What is missing in your life?

If the obsession were suddenly gone and you could never engage in it again, how big a hole would it leave in your life and what would you fill it with?

The Escape Test

Can you take a day off from your passion? Can you temporarily escape? Can you take two days off? Can you do something else without paying a price? If the answer to any of these questions is, "No, I can't," then the activity may contain at least an element of obsession. So the next question is, are you willing to change, and what might be in it for you to make this change?

The next chapter might help you answer that question as we take a closer look at what it really means to be rewarded by living your passions fully and in harmony with the rest of your life.

CHAPTER 8

Really Living What You Love

Elvis Presley danced, cavorted, and sang his way through several passions in his lifetime, including karate, women, rock and roll, and gospel singing in the wee hours of the morning in his Las Vegas penthouse. Trusted members of his entourage were instructed to invite one or more female fans to wait in a back bedroom in case Elvis grew tired of harmonizing with his backup singers and felt moved to engage one of his other passions.

Howard Buffett, the fifty-seven-year-old son of billionaire Warren Buffett, uses his fortune and influence to pursue several passions. Buffett, who is slated to inherit oversight of his father's Berkshire Holding Company, says he only agreed to accept that responsibility on condition that he was able to continue his daily, hands-on work on his fifteen-hundred-acre Illinois corn and soybean farm. He says he does his own planting and harvesting, a passion he acquired as a teenager when he found he loved "digging in dirt better than going to school." More recently he has initiated, funded, and led a training program for five thousand poor farmers in Africa, personally traveling there to teach them planting and harvesting techniques to improve the quality of their corn and bean crops. "That's what I'm really passionate about," Buffett says, "passing on what I know about farming."

Former Apple founder and CEO Steve Jobs said at his Stanford commencement address soon after he was diagnosed with pancreatic cancer, "Almost everything—all external expectations, all pride, all fear of embarrassment or failure—these things just fall away in the face of death, leaving only what is truly important. Remembering that you are going to die is the best way I know to avoid the trap of thinking you have something to lose. You are already naked. There is no reason not to follow your heart."

All three men—Presley, Buffett, and Jobs—achieved fame and fortune as a result or byproduct of their talent and the pursuit of their passions. Following passion doesn't usually garner fame and fortune, and it doesn't have to. For many, that's just not the main attraction. The research shows that the pursuit is its own reward.

In this chapter, we're going to have you do another passion assessment based on what we describe as the four dimensions of passion, which will reveal to you whether you're really living your passion. We'll also talk about the external and internal rewards of passion and why it's necessary to have both in order to experience real passion.

The Four Dimensions of Passion

Try this passion assessment yourself. Think of a passion you have or once had and then rate your engagement in that passion on the following four passion dimensions:

Complete the ratings that follow:

Passion (Name your passion here)

1. Intensity of interest in the activity (How interested in this passion are you?)

None to Low			Somewhat			High
1	2	3	4	5	6	7

An intensity rating of 1 equals no interest, and a rating of 7 indicates a very intense interest. Low interest in something you say is important to you or that you are passionate about can be a common sign of depression. You may be skimming the surface of life with little pleasure or satisfaction, even when you say something is important or a passion for you.

2) Immersion in the activity (How actively engaged or immersed are you in a typical passion experience?)

None to Low			Somewhat			High
1	2	3	4	5	6	7

When conductor Benjamin Zander conducts the Boston Philharmonic Orchestra in Gustav Mahler's Second Symphony, he frowns, jabs his finger, leans in and out, and sways from side to side on his pedestal. He is so fully and intently immersed in his passion for conducting that his movements are often as entertaining as the music he conducts.

Thankfully for those on the Boston Parkway after a Zander concert, the maestro is not quite as immersed and animated while driving home and listening to the Second Symphony on his car stereo. Total immersion is not always ideal—as with conducting an orchestra while driving—but full immersion is both a quality of passion and a characteristic of "flow," which we've mentioned before and which we will examine more closely in Chapter 13.

3) Frequency (How often do you engage in this passion?)

None to Low			Somewhat		High	
1	2	3	4	5	6	7

Maestro Zander, who is as passionate about teaching classical music as he is about conducting it, identified three groups of classical music listeners in his TED talk, which you can see on YouTube. He told his listeners that he suspected that only forty-five of more than a thousand people in the audience were "absolutely passionate" about classical music. By that, what he meant was "Your FM is always tuned to the classic station. You carry classical CDs in your car. Your children play a musical instrument—or you wish they did. You just can't imagine life without classical music."

A second, considerably larger group identified by Zander were those who "didn't mind" a little classical music once in a while—they were the ones who thought a glass of wine and a little Vivaldi in the background couldn't do any harm, but they didn't intently listen or enjoy the music. Then there was the third group, the largest, who almost never listened to classical music unless someone else dragged them to a concert. They never played it at home or in their car; classical music simply was not part of their life.

But even within the "very passionate" group, Zander saw a wide range of individual differences. Some rarely listened to classical music at home but always listened while driving to and from work. Some always had Bach, Vivaldi, or Mozart playing somewhere in the background. Others did so on occasion. The difference, in Zander's view, was frequency—how often during a typical day or week or year was classical music—or any particular passion—part of someone's experience.

4) Duration (How long is each passion experience on each occasion?)

None to Low			Somewhat			High
1	2	3	4	5	6	7

Looking back on his life, singer and entertainer Johnny Cash told the story of how he spotted a cheap guitar in a dime-store window when he was seven years old, persuaded his father to buy it for him, and had a guitar by his side ever after that first one.

"I slept with one for a while," he said. "A guitar was always with me." There is a classic photo of Cash as a teenager, ambling down a sidewalk with his instrument slung over his back. "My dream was to play and sing on the radio," he said. "So when I got out of the Air Force in 1954, that's what I did. I came back to Memphis and started knocking on radio station doors," carrying the guitar that had "worn my fingers down" in the service.

Cash said he practiced every free moment in the army. "That's why I kept my instrument close by," he said. "So I could learn." He says he often stayed back in the barracks alone, slipping out for a quick meal in the mess hall and then returning and practicing more. Some would argue that the amount of time Cash spent practicing was exceedingly long and obsessive. But so what? He had nothing else he felt passionate about at the time, and his later accomplishments were the result of all that practice learning his craft. Passions often do take time, especially in their early stages. The telling questions are (1) How much time is spent? and (2) Is there a cost in terms of time not spent in developing relationships and other important aspects of life? That's what we began to explore in the last chapter when we looked at the difference between obsessive and harmonious passions.

Most passions don't consume the amount of time Johnny Cash initially devoted to learning to play the guitar. The intensity, immersion, frequency, and duration may certainly vary with each of your passions, and that doesn't necessarily mean some are a lot more important than others. But being aware of these four dimensions of passion can help you to balance or harmonize some of your passions. For example, sometimes Bruce gets so lost in writing that his wife has to remind him to turn the computer off and spend a little time with her. He's learned to set an alarm on his computer. Evenings are set aside as "no-write time," a time reserved just for his wife Nancy and him to be together, a mutually shared passion.

Internal and External Rewards of Passion

Living one's passions delivers two kinds of returns: (1) internal, for the inherent in-the- moment pleasure of the activity itself, along with the satisfaction of completion; and (2) external—the praise, recognition, or other reward one sometimes receives from outside oneself.

Imagine an adolescent girl, for example, excitedly watching as her favorite female rock star lip-syncs her latest hit on MTV. Then she decides to learn to play the guitar, much like Johnny Cash did, as a prelude to a singing career leading to her own fame and fortune. Her initial reward and her motivation for spending her allowance on an instrument is purely internal. She imagines herself onstage, the strobe lights blinking and swirling around her, and the audience up on their feet, dancing in the aisles and singing the words of her latest single. It is that internal image that provides her with the initial incentive to take those first few steps toward mastering her passion, and maybe toward stardom. Does she truly know it will happen? She doesn't have to. Like a constant mega-buck-lottery ticket buyer, all she has to do is believe in the possibility to create an excited state of mind that provides its own reward.

The inevitable challenge for our hopeful singer is that she has to actually take the trouble to learn how to play a guitar, or at least a few chords—enough to blend in with her future backup band. Singing itself is not a problem. She already sings in the shower, which, in that environment, sounds at least as good as Lady Gaga.

So she buys her guitar—nylon strings, not metal (metal hurts the fingertips)—opens to page 2 in Guitar for Dummies, settles the lip of her instrument on her knee, and attempts to finger the G chord with her first, second, and third fingers. Her first five strums result in dead plunks, but then, on her sixth attempt, she hears a "TWAAANGGG," a perfect G-chord harmony. She grins. The sound pleases her. The reward—the harmonic sound—is entirely intrinsic. There's no one else in the room. She gets no praise or applause or nod of approval. There is no monetary reward. It actually cost a large part of her allowance to get that far, and even with nylon strings, her fingertips already hurt. Nonetheless, she is pleased. Her accomplishment feels good.

She fingers another G-chord. After a few more plunks, she twangs another perfect G-chord three times in a row, then glances up and smiles. She has taken her first few steps toward fame and fortune. After all, Lady Gaga is not as young as she used to be, and the industry will eventually need a replacement. Our novice guitar player's imagination has not only spurred her to envision a successful music career but has motivated her to work on the "hard part" of learning to play.

Now she stands up, leaves the room, and corners the first lucky person she runs across to excitedly demonstrate what she's learned. She sits down on a step or a bench, fingers a G-chord, strums a decent-sounding G-chord, and looks up with a question across her brow. Her mother, her father, her boyfriend, or whomever she's waylaid, stretches a genuine smile and says, "That's good. That's very good. I like it." That human feedback—assuming it's positive—is an external reward for her efforts, one that she sought and received.

We can probably assume that Lady Gaga still gets both internal and external rewards for her efforts. She probably doesn't need any more ready cash, so why does she continue to sing, record, and perform? On a radio interview she said, "I am a walking piece of art every day, with my dreams and my ambitions forward at all times in an effort to inspire my fans to lead their life in that way. Every bit of me is devoted to love and art, and I aspire to try to be a teacher to my young fans who feel just like I felt when I was younger. I just felt like a freak. I guess what I'm trying to say is I'm trying to liberate them. I want to free them of their fears and make them feel that they can make their own space in the world."

Her rewards are both external (fame and fortune bestowed by others) and internal (her ability to liberate her fans so they may "make their own space in the world"). She is passionate about performing and helping others, certainly a winning formula for her success.

That type of experience-over-acquisition reward is

supported by a number of studies that found "consistently higher happiness ratings for experiential purchases over material ones." A parallel nationwide survey of 1,279 adults between the ages of twenty-one and sixty-nine again favored experience over acquisition.

In one study, psychologists Todd Kashdan and William Breen found that "being preoccupied with the pursuit of money, wealth, and material possessions arguably fails as a strategy to increase pleasure and meaning in life. Our results indicate that people with stronger materialistic values report more negative emotions, less relatedness, less autonomy, competence, and gratitude." These experimenters concluded that "individuals who invest in experiences are happier than those who invest in material possession. More fun, less stuff!"

The combined results of these studies support the conclusion that uncovering and engaging in a passion is more fulfilling and longer lasting than buying something related to a passion. The satisfaction is not found in the buying or acquiring. It's found in the active engagement—in really using what's acquired.

The Best of Both

So what does this mean for those of us who may never acquire fame or fortune or accumulate more possessions than we could possibly use? We can take solace in the fact that, like love, money alone can't buy happiness. Statistics show that although the average income has risen over the past fifty years, happiness has remained flat.

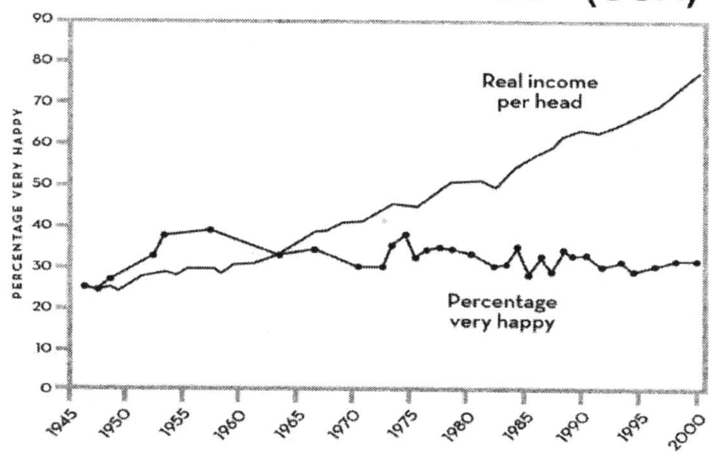

March 2010, *Sust. Degrowth w Amateur Econ.*, Degrowth Conference 2010, Barcelona — Jorgen S. Nørgård, Techn. Univ. of Denmark, DK2800 Lyngby, Denmark, jsn@byg.dtu.dk

If you think of your ultimate dream car, for example, and then close your eyes and imagine yourself driving that car on a beautiful coastal highway on a warm spring day, you probably envision yourself happily driving that car, especially if you have an abiding passion for cars. Buying the car and leaving it in the garage just doesn't spike the same degree of satisfaction. It's the experience of visualizing or actually engaging in your passion for driving that produces the rush.

Similarly, if you imagine yourself sitting on the deck of your dream vacation home, looking out across a lake or an ocean vista with a cup of tea or a cocktail in your hand as the sun slowly sets, it's hard to imagine yourself in that picture without a glimmer of satisfaction curling your lips into a smile. Simply buying that vacation home and owning it but never spending time there doesn't arouse the same satisfaction. Yet more vacation homes sit empty than not.

Acquisitions may create opportunities for experience. If driving, guitar playing, or trout fishing are already passions—

or could be—then owning a certain amount of paraphernalia might be a prerequisite for active engagement in those passions. But owning the paraphernalia is still not the same as really playing the guitar, driving, or trout fishing. When you look over your shoulder at life at some point down the road, you'll recall and savor those moments and experiences that your owning the equipment allowed to happen, often forgetting the particular set of oars or gulf clubs involved—unless you're one of those equipment geeks who is truly passionate about the technical aspects of using the equipment. The point is, it's more often the whole experience that leaves the afterglow.

It's often advised, "Follow your passion and the rewards will follow." There's no 100-percent guarantee in that, although it's certainly true that external rewards alone—that is, rewards without passion—won't result in satisfaction or a happy life. The best life, of course, combines internal satisfaction with external rewards, with a strong emphasis on the internal, for that will mean the most when the equipment is worn out, rusted, and long forgotten.

CHAPTER 9

Six Big Benefits to Living Your Passions

While the stories we shared in the previous chapter may be enough to inspire you to live your passions, we'd like now to share with you our experience of the extraordinary rewards of doing so.

Bruce always asks for feedback after a Passion Discovery workshop. He wants to know what worked and how to improve the experience the next time around. Six major areas have emerged as benefits of increased passion—although they're not the same for everyone and don't have the same order of importance. These benefits include (1) a laser-focused attention on the pursuit of passion, (2) a boost in energy, (3) expanded creativity, (4) a heightened sense of purpose, (5) a focus on improved health and self-care, and (6) an increase in self-esteem and optimism.

Let's look at each of these in greater detail, for as Marci Shimoff—close friend of Janet Attwood and the best-selling author of Happy for No Reason (2009)—said in an online interview, "When you live your passion, you are more in touch with the truth of who you are. When you find and follow your passion, you discover who you are and who you can be."

1. Passion Promotes Laser-Focused Attention on Best Performance

Earl Nightingale, the motivational speaker and voice of the old-time radio program Sky King, used to say in his well-attended talks, "The more intensely we feel about an idea or a goal, the more assuredly the idea, buried deep in our subconscious, will direct us along the path to its fulfillment."

Passion inspires the best in you because, if you're feeling passionate about something, if you love it, you're likely to want to do your best at it. Once discovered and nurtured, a passion directs your attention down a focused track, headed in a purposeful, self-chosen direction. You never know precisely where that track is leading. You might explore offshoots and even careen off in a new direction at some point, but you'll never spin in directionless circles or stay stuck in a rut.

2. *Passion Increases Energy and Inspires Action*

Passion energizes. As Donald Trump once said, "Without passion you don't have energy, and without energy you have nothing." Passion not only fires up your engines, it radiates from you and motivates others around you. Others see your glow and want to follow you. However one feels about Donald Trump, there is no denying he is one who lives and breathes "the deal."

One of Bruce's clients, Barbara, sought therapy because she said she was bored with herself and "bored with life." She then added, "I used to have a life." When he asked her what she meant by that, she said she had worked most of her adult life as a furniture and equipment buyer for the federal government, a job that had challenged her and that she had once loved.

"And now?" Bruce asked.

"I just go to the office and wait until the end of the day to go home."

By the time Barbara came for therapy, her mood had sunk from passionately engaged to chronically depressed.

Barbara had grown up in a small town in rural Pennsylvania and had never been particularly interested in school. She had always dreamed of moving away and living and working in the "excitement of the big city." After graduation, she followed a high school friend who had been recruited as a clerk-typist for the federal government in the Department of Commerce in Washington, DC.

"As it turned out," she told Bruce, "the big city was a little too big." She said she missed the closeness of small-town living, exactly what she had found "stifling" while growing up. But she said things changed for the better when she met Matt, a trainee in the Human Resources Department who took an interest in her and agreed to marry her after he got her pregnant.

Two children and a few years later, when Matt's parents retired and moved to their second home in Florida, they sold Matt and Barbara their three-acre home on the Eastern Shore of Maryland "for a song," Barbara said. "This was something we could never have afforded on our own. We just couldn't turn it down."

But there were certain disadvantages of Eastern Shore living, one of which was driving the seventy-five miles to work every day. Barbara said that Matt didn't mind the nearly two-hour commute into Washington. He revived his former passion for crime novels and listened to audiobooks during the ride. She said there were mornings he couldn't wait to get out the door and climb in the car to start again where he had left off with his latest thriller.

"It was a lot harder for me," Barbara said. "I hated the traffic. I hated the drive. I hated all of it. It wore me down after a while and I fell into a depression. I guess that's why I'm here."

A large part of therapy is helping clients develop options of which they aren't initially aware. Bruce always jots a note in the file when something comes up that might be useful later. In delving into Barbara's history, she had said that she was the younger of two daughters and that she had been a lot closer to her father than her mother. "They were on the verge of divorce a couple of times," she said. "My sister was my mother's favorite. That left Dad and me. On Saturdays, when he went down to the driving range to hit a few balls, he took me along. He bought me a set of children's clubs and I got pretty good. The ball started to go where I aimed it most of the time."

"And did you?" Bruce asked.

"What?"

"Get to liking golf?"

"I guess."

Bruce wrote "golf" in the margin of his therapy notes. Over the next few sessions, as he got to know Barbara, other potential passions emerged during the course of her therapy that he thought might ignite a spark in her life. They talked about the passion she had once found in her job purchasing furniture, and the need to challenge herself emerged as a predominant theme.

Barbara made good progress and was slowly weaned off the antidepressant her family physician had prescribed. As part of her long-term treatment plan, she agreed to sign up for a four-week series of golf lessons at the local YMCA. Bruce knew her well enough to know that if she paid for the classes, she would take them, since she hated "wasting hard-earned money." She made a number of other changes in her life, but in the end, she said, "It was golf that got me out from under that cloud. Once I got started, it gave me something to work toward. It's not an easy game, and I love getting better at it."

Her long drives were more enlightening and enlivening as she listened to audio programs centering on golf—biographies of famous players, histories of the game, and how-to books. "I even started practicing just by thinking about it," she said. "I read in an article in Golf magazine that you could do that—that you could build muscle memory just thinking through the motions needed for a perfect swing."

Eight months later—two months after therapy ended—Bruce ran across Barbara at the local grocery store.

"I want to thank you," she said to him.

"For what?" Bruce asked.

"For giving me my life back. Golf wasn't all of it, but that's what gave me the boost I needed. It's amazing how taking a stick and poking a little ball in a little hole can make such a difference."

Psychologist and inspirational speaker Wayne Dyer, in one of his PBS television talks, said that passion is "the energy directed at the object of passion." It was Barbara's renewed passion for golf that helped overcome the drudgery of her daily commute. She said the drive seemed shorter with something to think about and that her renewed energy spread beyond golf to reignite her former passion for her work. Then once she got to work, "it started feeling like it used to."

Randy has also discovered that when he is able to help clients find and engage with even one passion, the excitement, energy, and focus can completely shift a person's overall life view to a more positive frame of reference. In psychology, we call that "generalization," whereby one thing begins to have multiple effects on other aspects of one's life. Once Barbara rediscovered a new love, she stopped hating her job.

3. Passion Ignites Interest, Exploration, and Creativity

Wayne Dyer also said in one of his TV talks, "When passion is renewed, options seem to come along and open up." They do. When you are passionate about something, your eyes and ears—all your senses—are open to opportunities to engage that interest. Research indicates that you're less tense with passion in your life and freer to notice and respond to possibilities as they open up before you. As Oprah Winfrey once confessed, she sometimes didn't feel like going out in front of the cameras and doing another show, but as soon as she was out there and involved, as soon as she felt passionate about the subject and her guest, she could feel the energy bubbling up inside her and she knew the audience felt the same. Passion is at the heart of Oprah's success. She passionately cares, and we feel her passion and join her as she lives her passions full out.

Here are two other cases of lost passion that illustrate the effects of uncovering new passions and reigniting and living old passions in a new way.

Putting a Life Back Together

The first is another story from Bruce about a client who turned his life around in a Passion Discovery process that began with loss.

Jerry, a client I treated for depression after his wife died in an auto accident, returned years later saying that he hadn't relapsed—therapy and time had done their job—but he still wasn't sure what he wanted to do with his life and wondered if he should return to therapy. At the time, I was about to start a Passion Discovery workshop and thought that might be a better alternative. If not, I told him we could reconsider therapy.

Jerry was an administrator for the Department of Education who drove from his home in Easton, on Maryland's Eastern Shore, to Annapolis every day. Unlike Barbara (in the previous story), Jerry enjoyed the drive. He told the class that it "gives me a chance to think. It's a nice break between home and work."

"Can you tell everyone why you're here, why you took the Passion Discovery class?" I asked.

"My wife died three years ago," he said. "It just hasn't been the same since. We were soulmates. We did so much together—nearly everything. Lately, I've been feeling at loose ends and looking for something to do."

The class had no response. They weren't sure what to say. But as they got to know Jerry over the next few weeks, it was obvious that many who came felt a great deal of warmth and affection toward him.

In one of Jerry's Passion Discovery exercises, he wrote and then shared with the class that he and his wife had always enjoyed watching seasonal changes and the migration of waterfowl as they passed through the wetlands around their home. They had once considered researching migration patterns but had never gotten much further. "We bought a lot of books and talked about it, but that's as far as it went."

Birding was only one of the activities on Jerry's emerging passion list, but that was the one he homed in on. The question was, would it be too painful and would it remind him too much of his wife?

"I think it's a good thing," a class member blurted out when Jerry expressed his misgivings. "I'm sorry," she quickly added when the rest of the class turned to face her.

"No, go ahead," Jerry said. "What do you mean?"

"Well, I just think, what would she want? How could you do something that she would want you to do? Something that maybe you could do in memory of her. Something that your memory of her would add to your life, not take away."

That idea inspired Jerry. He told the class the following week that he had parked along the side of the road and gotten out to watch a flock of migrating geese squawking and flapping their wings overhead. "You know the beautiful part?" he said. "I thought of Marie. It was as if she were standing right there next to me."

Jerry considered several potential passions during the workshop, but he realized that birding was something he could build a new life around while recalling fond memories of his time with Marie. He never asked for therapy after the class ended. He didn't need it.

Psychiatry, Politics, and Murder Mysteries

One of the most creative results of a Passion Discovery experience happened unexpectedly when Bruce met a psychiatrist named John at a convention in Las Vegas. The two happened to sit at the same lunch table and began discussing their mutual interests, including passion—a subject that often turns personal, as it did on that occasion.

John had earned his undergraduate degree from New York University and then went onto medical school at Columbia before studying psychiatry at the Jungian Institute in Switzerland. "I guess you could say I saw the world a little differently in those days," he told Bruce. "I was interested in the inner world, my own. I was my own patient."

John partnered with another Jungian Institute graduate,

and together they ran a successful joint practice in San Francisco for years. "The truth is," he said, "I started feeling drained a few years ago. Every time another patient left the couch, they took a little piece of me with them. After a while, there wasn't much left."

As they continued to speak, John expressed an interest in the work Bruce was doing with passion and asked if he could try some of the Passion Discovery exercises. Bruce said yes, and after they returned to their respective homes, Bruce e-mailed John similar exercises to the ones included in Chapters 3 and 4. As he finished each exercise, he e-mailed his answers for thoughts and comments.

In the "looking back" exercise, John realized that he had spent his entire adult life in and around big cities, but at heart he felt most comfortable and at home in the small, upstate New York town where he'd grown up. "Smallville," he wrote in an e-mail. "I couldn't wait to get out of there. But at this point in my life, I guess I'd like the peace and quiet. I miss knowing everyone."

In a subsequent exercise, when asked for his best memory of "Smallville," he e-mailed that he recalled spending Saturday mornings sitting in the waiting-room chair of his Uncle Harry's barbershop while his father, the town physician, made his rounds at the local hospital. "You know what I liked most about that?" John asked rhetorically, then immediately answered it. "I liked getting to know all the men in town. Some better than those on my therapist's couch in San Francisco."

John developed a robust list of potential passions, some of which had never occurred to him before because he had never taken the time to systematically consider the possibilities. He thanked Bruce and then was out of touch for over a year. In the next e-mail Bruce received from John, the subject line read:

"New Psychiatrist in Smallville."

How creative, Bruce thought as he read it. While John slowly weaned his long-term patients off therapy and referred others on to his partner, he began taking more trips back home, sitting on front porches and talking to longtime neighbors and those he newly met. Many were concerned about how the town was dying, with many stores bolting their doors for good or moving out to the new shopping center on the highway. "I got interested in the town as a grownup," he wrote. "I wanted to do what I could to preserve the best part of small-town living. I realized that could be a passion for me and maybe help bring a little life back to me and to the town. Just talking to people, I already had lots of ideas."

As it turned out, John wasn't tired of seeing patients. He was tired of seeing too many, and at this point in his life, he didn't need to. Over the course of his career in psychiatry, he had prudently saved his money and had done fairly well with his investments. By the time I heard from him again, he had moved back to Smallville, started a part-time practice, and been elected to the town council.

As it turns out, writing a mystery novel with a psychiatrist as the leading character was another item on John's passion list. "I've already blocked out a plot and have written the first few chapters," he e-mailed Bruce. "It feels like I'm starting a new life. It is a new life." Acting on and living his renewed passion for small-town living had spurred John's creativity in many ways.

4. Passion Boosts a Sense of Meaning and Purpose

The meaning of life, or the meaning of anything, doesn't exist in a vacuum. Meaning is embedded in something else, and that something is embedded in something else. Author and radio host Mitch Albom writes in his book Have a Little Faith (2009), "The way you get meaning into your life is to devote yourself to loving others, devote yourself to your community around you, and devote yourself to creating something that gives you purpose and meaning." Actor James Earl Jones said, "Love is just a word until someone comes along and gives it meaning."

Meaning of a Higher Order

For those who are religious, the big meaning of life may be embedded in the word of God, Allah, Krishna, Vishnu, Maheshvar, Rama—or Adi Purusha, the Timeless Being. Such people's purpose and ultimate meaning is found in a Supreme Being's divine law. The Qur'an, for example, commits the Muslim faithful to five pillars of faith: (1) following the Islamic creed as established by God's dictation to Mohammed and later written down, (2) engaging in daily prayer, (3) fasting during Ramadan, (4) giving alms to the poor, and (5) making a pilgrimage to Mecca at least once in a lifetime if at all possible. Following these tenets can become a passion for those who embrace this world religion.

One of the tenets of Christianity—as exemplified by Mother Teresa, Martin Luther King Jr., and many others—is to devote your life to the service of others, particularly to the oppressed and less fortunate, as exemplified by Jesus' caring for the poor and the outcast. There's no doubt that many religious faithful passionately devote their lives to what they consider to be their divinely inspired mission, and they derive deep personal meaning from pursuing that mission.

In an online article posted by the Hartford Institute for

Religion Research, Ronald Sider, the institute's director, writes that "religious meaning rests on a perception of the good that God intends for persons and communities, and on the belief that God enlists Christians to respond to need and injustice by working toward different social realities. A personal mandate for activism may derive from scripture, from church leaders, or from inner spiritual guidance."

Mark Bradshaw, a psychologist and an excellent therapist who worked for Bruce as a staff psychologist at a community mental health center, once approached him with a professional and religious dilemma. Mark was a devout Methodist and a lay preacher at a local Methodist Church, as well as a Little League coach for the church-sponsored team. He was passionate about his religious calling but felt stymied when he was not legally or ethically permitted to administer Christian counseling to the mentally ill in a secular state facility.

Bruce hated to lose Mark, but he had no trouble knowing what to do. He wrote a glowing but honest recommendation that helped Mark get a job as a psychologist at a Christian mental health clinic in Des Moines, Iowa—a long way from Maryland but an intensely personal journey that allowed Mark to follow his passionate religious calling and his profession at the same time.

In this case, it's important for one to discover the best environment in which multiple passions can be lived so that maximum fulfillment and meaning are achieved.

To Some It Is Given

A dorm-mate of Bruce at Stanford University had his own unique approach to religious passion. He agreed that religion infused a believer with meaning, passion, and purpose but argued that the fire of religious passion could just as easily grease a slippery slide to the gates of hell as build a stairway to heaven.

He liked to use the example of Sir Thomas More, the one-time "religious and moral advisor" to King Henry VIII of England who burned Christians at the stake for not following his particular brand of Christianity. After personally ordering their deaths, More watched dozens torched while he stood in silence, his expression stern, his hands locked behind his back. As karma would have it, Sir Thomas More met death when his religious views crossed those of King Henry VIII, since both men were obsessed with killing those who didn't believe as they did.

Religious belief is clearly one path to meaning and purpose. Those who believe are lucky. Their purpose and direction are given. All they have to do is follow their beliefs. For another group, the entire concept of meaning is irrelevant. They simply live their lives and don't think much about it. Others wrestle with meaning but never pin it down. What is important, however, and what we do know through psychological research, is that those who have no passions of any kind or don't pursue their passions, religious or non-religious, lead a far less fulfilling life than those who do. It is our passions—the things we love and believe in, the things we look forward to—that fill our lives with purpose and meaning. We'll talk more about the role of meaning in sustaining one's passion in Chapter 15, "Meaning and Passion."

5. Passion Is Good for Health and May Promote Longer Life

Bruce tells this heartwarming story about living one's

passion nearer the end of life:

I once worked as a therapist in a Delaware nursing home, where most of the residents were all too aware that they were there to die—that this place would be their last. I wasn't surprised that many were depressed. More intriguing, however, were those who weren't depressed, some of whom seemed to actually thrive there—rolling up and down the corridors, smiling and braking their wheelchairs to chat with anyone they could waylay for a moment or two.

When I accepted the job, I knew from teaching Lifespan Psychology that maintaining passion at the end of life was highly correlated with both health and longevity. In one long-term study of 180 nuns, 90 percent of those who frequently expressed passion and positive emotions in their writings lived to age eighty-five or beyond. Over half of them lived to age ninety-four. In contrast, only 34 percent of the less passionate nuns lived to age eighty-five, and only 11 percent lived to ninety-four.

On one of my regular Thursday nursing home visits, the head nurse asked me to walk down the hall to evaluate an eighty-three-year-old resident, Agnes, who refused to leave her room or talk to anyone. Agnes didn't talk to me either, not initially, and I didn't require it. Instead, I slowly entered her room, allowing her plenty of personal space as I watched her lower her chin and partially close her eyes, pretending to ignore me.

"Hello, Agnes," I said in a quiet voice. "I'm the psychologist here. I know we haven't met. I just came down to introduce myself."

I waited and then added, "I'm here every Thursday. I'll come back to see you again, if you don't mind."

I didn't expect a nod or a sign of recognition, and I

didn't get one. But I did have a chance to glance around her room, and I noticed a framed photograph of what appeared to be a family standing on a boardwalk at a beach—a man and woman in bathing suits with a young girl leaning in at the mother's side, maybe six or seven, and a boy a year or two older grinning into the camera at the father's side.

When I wandered back to the nursing station and inquired, I was told that Agnes' daughter had brought the photograph in on one of her rare visits from California. The nurse told me that she wasn't sure about the boy in the picture—as far as she knew, a son had never visited—but that the daughter said the family had once lived near the beach in Delaware.

I had a daughter about the age of the girl in the photograph. On my next visit, I slowly entered Agnes's room again. I waited and then said, "I have a daughter, too. I worry about her sometimes. I'll bring a picture next time, if that's OK."

I brought the photograph on the following Thursday, and that was the key that initially unlocked the door to Agnes's trust. "I lost everything," she told me on my fourth visit. "My husband. The house. My mind even. I can't remember things like I used to."

For most of her life, Agnes had been the only librarian in a small-town library. "I helped raise a lot of the kids in that town," she told me. "Their parents dropped them off at story time and left them there to read for hours."

I thought about Agnes as I drove back and forth to the facility. She could obviously never again be a librarian—a passion to which she had once devoted her life. "I can still read with my glasses," she said. "I just can't remember. I have to keep turning back and reading again."

I had slowly won her trust but had found no reason yet to wedge her out of her room and wheel her chair down the long nursing home corridor.

"She's wasting away," the physical therapist told me. "She gets no exercise at all. She hardly eats."

I knew from over a hundred studies on passion that 85 percent of individuals say they have a "moderate passion" for at least one activity. When I met Agnes, she had no passion for anything, although her life had been full of passion for books and reading, and for encouraging others to share her passion. "I used to travel the world," she said on one of our visits. "Without ever leaving the library."

As most therapists would, I was fishing for something to catch her interest and lure her out of the doldrums. Her passion for running a library was the bait I needed. "I wonder if maybe you could help me?" I asked, after she began to look forward to our visits. "All those big-print books down in the dayroom are a mess. Nobody can find anything. Those who read at all just toss them back anywhere. Do you think you could do me a favor? Could you take a look and see what could be done? I'd do it myself, but I have no idea where to begin."

Agnes was on to my ruse, but we had established a good therapeutic relationship and she knew I cared about her. Once I got her out into the hall and down to the day-room, we slowly reignited her passion for helping others. After several weeks, she volunteered for the unpaid position of "part-time nursing home librarian," a job that needed doing. "Someone has to," she told me.

As Agnes's mood gradually improved, she joined the wheelchair exercise group and began eating better and gaining a little weight. Her reignited passion for books and helping others may lengthen her life. More important, it clearly improved her health and her quality of life right away. On my final day at the nursing home, when I went down to the new library center to say good-bye, she reached up from her wheelchair, yanked me down, hugged me, and planted a kiss on my cheek. "Thanks" she said, and recommended the latest best seller as something I might enjoy.

6. Passion Just Feels Good

A life without passion can be a dull life. Studies have shown that passion is highly correlated with a number of measures of joy, contentment, and a sense of well-being. There are lots of reasons for engaging in a new passion or old ones, not the least of which is that it's just more fun. You feel better when you're passionately involved with something you love. And that's probably the underlying reason that Chris Attwood, co-author of The Passion Test book, ends up with "having fun" in his top five passions every time he takes the test. He, like most of us, likes to feel good as much of the time as possible.

In Randy's therapy practice of years past, he'd notice that people would say they were sick and tired of being sick and tired but not sure where to go with that. It's true that you have to want to feel better. Some seem addicted to melancholy or feeling the blues, as it's familiar and comfortable. And they don't have to change. When people are finally ready to move out of that state of chronic blues, discovering or rediscovering passion is certainly one of the first antidotes to apply.

CHAPTER 10

Living Passion in Relationships

As humans, we need other humans. We couldn't survive without them—certainly not at birth and for a good number of years after. We need their protection. We need their comfort, their warmth, and their sustenance. That initial life-or-death parental connection bonds us for life, so it's not surprising that relationships are a crucial factor in overall life satisfaction.

As Woody Allen said to his psychiatrist in the movie Annie Hall, "It was great seeing Annie again. I realized what a terrific person she was and how much fun it was just knowing her. And I thought of that old joke, y'know, this guy goes to a psychiatrist and says, 'Doc, my brother's crazy; he thinks he's a chicken.' And the doctor says, 'Well, why don't you turn him in?' The guy says, 'I would, but I need the eggs.' Well, I guess that's pretty much now how I feel about relationships. Y'know, they're totally irrational, and crazy, and absurd, and . . . but I guess we keep goin' through it because, uh, most of us need the eggs."

In an interview for the Denver Post, psychologist Michael Steger said that his research on the importance of meaning in life found that relationships were an important component of meaning. "Depending on the stages of life," Steger said, "those relationships can be parents or extended family. People value us, they interest us, and help us grow. They carry on a legacy, they give us a sense of our place in time."

But what do close relationships—especially living-together relationships—have to do with passion? Quite a lot. Passions among friends and lovers are often an important part of their relationship. It's hard to imagine a close relationship that has no common passions. One of those passions is a passion for each other—you spend a lot of time together, you enjoy each other's company, and the relationship is a strong part of how you define yourself. Of course, when you're not getting along, it's hard to share passions and feel passionate. The better you get along, the more likely shared passions will fill your together-life and the more likely you will support each other in your separate passions.

In this chapter, we'll explore the role that mutual passions and interests play in relationships. Shared passions can be an essential for choosing a partner, and rediscovering mutual interests can save a partnership.

It's also helpful to understand differences between men and women in the context of relationship, and to ensure that a relationship succeeds, it's extremely supportive to understand the importance of the five-to-one ratio of positive to negative comments. Understanding that every member of a family has the right to live his passion can have a profound effect on each member and that family as a whole.

All of these topics are discussed in this chapter.

Passing the Possibilities Test

Every unmarried single searching for his or her near-perfect mate on Match.com knows that intimate relationships are often ignited in the heat of erotic passion but that they survive on the understanding and warmth of shared passions and interests.

Cyberspace is jammed on weeknights with singles in search of their near-perfect match to meet up with on Friday or Saturday evening, well aware that their slightly-less-than-perfect match is online in search of them. The first thing a match-dot-comer does is type in a preferred age somewhat close to his own. He then scans smiling photographs with the understanding that it's common for each potential match to post a slightly younger face and shave a few years off his actual age.

Our match-dot-comer is hoping for someone at least as handsome or as attractive as he is—and with any luck, a notch above. Next, education and occupation are scanned to see if his potential match can hold a decent conversation and if the person has financial resources that at least match his own. Those lucky few still remaining on the hold-as-possibilities list are scrutinized again with a keen eye and sharper judgment. The top three or four are then e-mailed, and if all that goes well, a face-to-face meeting is arranged for a quick coffee and an easy escape.

But all that is just the preliminaries. The crunch comes at the meeting. First, there's the visual check. Photos lie, especially when they're ten or fifteen years younger than the person sitting across the table. If what our match-dot-comer sees lights up the room, his next thought is, Let's talk politely for half an hour or so and see where this goes.

Assuming all those hurdles are cleared, the real test comes in the next two parts. The first question is, what kind of a relationship is the other person looking for? If our match-dot-comer and this other person were to fall madly in love, would this person be capable of a close relationship? So our match-dot-comer ask questions like: "So tell me, have you been married before?" or "What happened to your last relationship?

Why did it end?" What he's probably looking for here is whether a previous breakup was the other person's fault, and if so, how does that bode for a relationship with him? If that test is passed, then it's on to the second test: what are their interests and passions? It's the results of this final probe, if all the other conditions are met, that will determine the long-term success of the relationship.

Randy likes to remind people seeking significant relationships that being clear about their passions before they find a partner helps them find that near-perfect match. He advises clients and audiences to ask themselves several questions to help them understand themselves and narrow down what they're looking for. These include the following:

What top five passions matter most in life to you?

What attributes or characteristics are you looking for in a partner?

What kinds of experiences do you most want to share with a partner?

What does your past experience teach you about what works in an effective, caring partnership?

What would you want your ideal partner to expect of you?

Shared Passions

Shared interests and passions may or may not form the magnet that initially draws two people together, but they do form one of the pillars that hold up a relationship as it continues to change and grow. A second pillar supporting a long-term relationship is a willingness to self-disclose—to share and reveal your likes and dislikes, your successes and failures, your goals and passions, your dreams and aspirations, and your innermost thoughts and feelings. If one person stops disclosing, the other is likely to shut down and stop disclosing as well. Continued self-disclosure is far easier when people have common interests and passions to share and discuss.

A third pillar of relationship success is a knack or skill for handling disagreements and differences in a way that doesn't chip away at the relationship's foundation. That's also easier in the context of a backlog of goodwill established through building trust, friendship, and common interests.

Togetherness

One way to deepen intimacy is to continually discover, uncover, and explore each other's interests and passions and then to develop common passions. One couple I know dressed up in their tennis outfits every Saturday morning and went out for a game after breakfast. But when I asked them how their game went, they confessed that they didn't really play a game. All they did was take turns hitting the ball across the net for as long as they could keep a volley going. They didn't keep score. They didn't want to end up with a winner and a loser. All they wanted to do was to get a little exercise and have a little fun together. As for another couple I knew, he had a passion for fishing and she had swum all her life, so they usually vacationed where they could both express their passions and then spend the evenings enjoying a good dinner and each other's company.

But what do you do if you're in a relationship where there are no common interests or passions? What if the initial passion that drew you together was purely erotic, and when that cooled, there wasn't much left? Or what if one person took a big leap in a different direction, seemingly leaving the other person behind? That mismatch is sometimes the reason a couple signs up for a Passion Discovery class. They're hoping to discover or develop common connections that will help them rebuild and strengthen their relationship.

Margi—half of the couple Margi and John—had played the viola ever since grade school and had always been in an amateur orchestra as an adult. John, an outdoorsman, had persuaded a reluctant Margi to invest in a $40,000 camper that they rarely used because Margi didn't like being "cooped up that long." Nor did she like taking lengthy road trips that interfered with her viola practice and orchestral rehearsals. After separately completing the Passion Discovery exercises, they rediscovered a mutual interest in nature, especially in botany, a college course they had both loved but that neither had pursued beyond college.

After a bit of negotiating, John agreed to plan their road trips around Margi's rehearsal and orchestra schedule. On occasion, he would spend time on the road alone, enjoying his independence while Margi arranged to fly into a local airport and join him later on the route. Their road time together would include planned visits to a botanical garden or a nature center. If they could arrange it, they would sign up for a workshop or a day course on some aspect of botany, planting, forestry, or wildlife management. "I don't know if this is going to work," John said at the end of their Passion Discovery experience, "but I feel like we're working together instead of pulling in opposite directions, trying to convince each other of the right way to do things."

Randy has found that couples who take the Passion Test workshop that he and Karin lead often end the day with a smile and a fresh glow as they look at each other after discovering new passions they can share and support in their growth together.

The Five Languages of Love

Randy and Karin frequently recommend therapist Gary Chapman's book, The Five Love Languages: The Secret to Love That Lasts (2009), for secrets on how to keep a relationship and marriage alive and fresh.

Chapman believes that each person has a "love cup," which can be filled or drained. Chapman's five primary means to express and receive love are gifts, words of affirmation, acts of service, quality time, and physical affection. We often give the kind of love we want to receive because that's the kind of love language we understand, instead of giving our partner what they want to receive—instead of speaking their language of love.

For instance, Randy's preferred ways of filling his love cup are quality time and acts of service. Karin's preferred love languages are physical affection and words of affirmation. When Randy spends time doing almost anything with Karin, he's content and happy. He loves it when Karin makes dinner for the two of them. When Karin receives loving physical affection from Randy, she's in relationship heaven. When Randy forgets to fill Karin's love cup in her language of love, her vitality and energy falter. She wilts.

Randy and Karin are now in their second quarter-century together, more and more speaking the language of love that each of them needs as they help others learn to do the same.

The Difference Between Men and Women

Repeated psychological studies of married heterosexual couples have shown that women tend to be more critical of husbands than husbands are of wives—that women often enter marriage hoping to change their husbands while men enter marriage hoping their wives will remain the same. For both sexes, however, criticism, disrespect, and disdain are the greatest predictors of marital failure.

As psychologist John Buri writes in How To Love Your Wife (2006), a self-help book for men, "If you want to destroy your marriage with one fell swoop—cheat. But if you want to slowly bludgeon a marriage to death—criticize." Buri also wrote a parallel book for women in which he suggests that "fixer-upper husbands" are never fully fixed and that a never-ending project to do so is an uphill battle and a downhill slide to relationship disaster. A "fix-'em-up" mentality chronically focuses on what's wrong and still needs fixing rather than an acceptance of imperfections and emphasis on what's good, right, and lovable.

George and Martha

There's a certain kind of overheated negative passion that should clearly be avoided in a relationship—particularly the sort of disrespect and anger spit from the sharp-tongued mouths of George and Martha in Edward Albee's play Who's Afraid of Virginia Woolf. It's a play in which marital partners taunt and tease each other mercilessly, picking at the worst of each other's faults in a sadomasochistic display of cruelty that marked their love-hate feelings for each other. Most relationships aren't nearly that vindictive or volatile, but gripes and grudges are often saved up to use as ammunition when one or the other "starts something."

Psychologist John Gottman has spent most of his career studying successful marriages and the ingredients that make them successful. After more than thirty years in the field, Gottman has determined that close to 70 percent of marital conflicts swirl around problems that are either personality differences or lifestyle preferences. The continual clashes in these two areas tend to build up and fester as each person tries to convince the other to change while neither budges—each of them thinking, If he/she loved me, he/she would simply do as I asked.

Gottman concluded from studying long-term "successfully happy couples" that "relationships work best to the extent they wind up with a set of perpetual problems that each learns to accept and live with." Gottman's advice? Don't expect perfection unless you have it to offer. Instead of resisting or fighting, try to understand why the other person is the way they are. If you can accept that and learn to live with what you consider his or her faults, you then have a right to ask them to live with what they consider to be your faults.

Forgiveness

Hard feelings and hurt feelings, saved up and carted around, form an increasingly heavy burden that eventually wears down even the most passionate relationships. When psychologists Frank Fincham and Steven Beach (2012) examined the connection between forgiveness and the quality of marital life, they found forgiveness to be "an effortful strategy to resolve relationship difficulties." It was "effortful forgiveness," combined with thoughtful negotiation, that allowed a couple to get beyond argumentative sticking points to start moving forward again.

The results of Fincham and Beach's study of heterosexual couples indicated, however, that women forgive more quickly than men, especially after a "relationship transgression." Men, rather than immediately forgiving and trying to work things out, were more likely to initially separate and emotionally withdraw. These researchers concluded that "women's propensity to forgive is predictive of both their own and their partner's future marital quality in a manner that is not true for a husband's propensity to forgive. Rather, for husbands, it is increased marital quality that appears to lead to a greater propensity to forgive."

In other words, when a woman forgives, the relationship immediately improves as a result of her forgiveness. A man, on the other hand, tends to forgive only after the relationship improves. Women forgive earlier, if they forgive at all, and their forgiveness allows them to work to improve the relationship. Men hold back on forgiveness until they are assured the relationship is improving.

Jennifer and Jim, after considering a separation, sought counseling in order to give their marriage "one more try." Jim had moved out of the house and in with his brother after he caught his wife "cheating with one of her colleagues." He said that everyone had been drinking at a Christmas party at someone's home when he noticed Jennifer missing. When he asked around, he was told that she was upstairs in one of the bedrooms with someone from work. When Jim found the door locked, he knocked and then banged. When no one answered, he left and drove home jealous and enraged. After following him in a borrowed car, Jennifer confessed to "a brief affair" with another teacher, and Jim packed a bag and stormed out.

"So why do you want to stay married?" Bruce asked Jim, when he saw them together in therapy.

"Because I still love her. I just can't get that picture out of my mind."

"Tell him the rest of it," Jennifer said.

"I'm not exactly guiltless myself," Jim confessed. "I told her I've been with two other women since we've been married. It was purely sexual. Nothing else. That's all it was."

"Why did you tell her?" asked Bruce.

"Because how could I accuse her of what I did myself?"

They had been married eight years and had a number of passions and interests in common. They both loved nature, the change of seasons, seafood, and boating on Chesapeake Bay. After they married, they saved up and bought a small house on the water and then had it torn down and replaced with what they called their dream home.

Besides a common love for Eastern Shore living, they shared a passion for opera. Every year they bought season tickets to the Kennedy Center Opera House in Washington, DC, and then drove into town for each performance, spending the night in their favorite small hotel. They were both teachers. Jennifer taught tenth-grade English at the county high school. Jim taught communication arts at the local community college. They loved their jobs and supported each other through long hours of grading papers, preparing for classes, and working with students. Before infidelity drove a wedge between them, they had been planning to start a family and were busy reading books on "how to raise the perfect child," as Jim put it. "Or as close as we could get."

There were other issues besides infidelity, but certainly not a lack of mutual interests and passions. In fact, that was a large part of the glue that held them together during their struggle over betrayal. They both agreed that they had built a good life together and wanted to find a way to get it back again.

Bruce told them to keep in mind that they couldn't change anything that had happened. If they wanted their relationship to work, they would have to forgive the past, get beyond hurt feelings, and move forward from there.

Forgiveness for infidelity is never easy, and it certainly wasn't for Jim and Jennifer. It took time for healing and for trust, once lost, to be regained. As expected, Jim took longer, but Jennifer was patient, doing more than her share until Jim let his guard down and began to open up and let her in again.

Small Forgiving

Forgiveness for a sexual transgression is a "Big Forgive." Most forgiveness is over little matters—differences of opinion, harsh words meant but not necessary, ignoring each other when love and support are needed. Unfortunately, not only do we inevitably notice the negatives more often, it's even worse. A disparaging remark is usually more trusted. When people say something negative to your face, they usually mean it. Compliments and praise, on the other hand, are meted out for lots of reasons, not all of them sincere.

But beyond believability, John Gottman's successful marriage research has found that negative comments hurt more, count for more, and leave a longer-lasting impact than positive comments. His research indicates that it takes five positive comments and gestures to balance out one negative. Gottman (2010) goes so far as to say that, if the positive-to-negative ratio falls below five-to-one, "the relationship is likely to fail and break up—that bad events are so much stronger than good ones that the good must far outnumber the bad in order to prevail."

It's hard enough to maintain a consistent five-to-one positive ratio when things are going well, partly because we tend to take the positives for granted and exaggerate the negatives. We may think positively but don't always say it out loud. It's when we notice something negative or irritating that we're more likely to point it out.

Butting Heads or Shaking Hands

So how do you maintain a five-to-one positive ratio and forgive the little things as the relationship moves along? Here are some suggestions:

Remind yourself that everyone is different, but not necessarily wrong. There will always be disagreements, differences of opinion, and moments of frustration between two people who live together, even when they care for each other, but it's not the differences that determine the long-term quality of the relationship. It's whether or not those differences are handled in a loving, caring way.

Be willing to negotiate and compromise. When a grudge is held, even the tiniest spark can reignite a simmering resentment. As resentments build, conflict is increasingly common. The research shows that forgiveness for small slights and indiscretions may be one of the more valuable tools for maintaining a healthy, loving, vibrant relationship. It's through forgiveness and looking for mutually satisfying solutions that understanding grows and the relationship is strengthened.

Repeat the Passion Discovery exercises or the Passion Test together every once in a while to sharpen and fortify your mutual passions and to support and encourage each other in your individual passions. Expanding common interests and passions is one way to continue to grow and thrive as individuals and as a couple. As both your lives change, continue to expand and grow together by reviewing and reconsidering your answers to the Passion Discovery exercises.

Every once in a while, keep a personal five-to-one positive monitoring record. Consider making a deliberate, conscious effort to monitor and record your positive-to-negative, strokes-to-pokes ratio. (Remember, it's not what you think is negative. It's what the other person takes as negative that counts.) Since negatives count five times more than positives, it's important to keep the positives high. One method to get you into that habit is to keep handy a simple 5 x 8 index card on which you put a checkmark every time you sincerely notice and compliment your loved one. ("Great dinner, dear." "Thanks for taking out the trash. I appreciate that." "It really helped when you noticed I was a little down and you talked to me about it.") Aim for five pluses each day for a week until you acquire the habit of noticing and communicating more positives.

State of the Union

In any relationship, when someone wants to discuss something, it's often something that they don't like or care for. In other words, it's often something negative. After all, why discuss what's not a problem—there's nothing to discuss. What needs discussing is what needs fixing or correcting. Unfortunately, when a corrective issue is brought up, the other person often feels accused and defensive, which either leads nowhere or leads to an offensive response like "OK then, here's what I don't like about you."

To get around defensive and counter-defensive moves and actually discuss and resolve issues, Gottman advises a regularly scheduled "state-of-the-union" meeting as a way to keep in touch and settle small issues before they mushroom into big ones. Here's how it works:

Agree on a specific time for a regular state-of-the-union meeting in a quiet place at a time when you can be sure you won't be interrupted.

At that meeting, decide who begins.

Before the person who begins can say anything negative (or even neutral), he or she is required to mention five instances in the last week that he or she sincerely liked, loved, or appreciated about the other person or about their relationship. (Considering the five-to-one positive-to-negative ratio, the starter has to earn an opportunity to say something that might be taken as negative.)

The person who starts must also state his or her concern or issue with as little blame as possible. ("I know I need a lot of attention," or "I know I can be quite messy in the kitchen when I'm in a hurry," etc.)

The listener simply listens and then, without defending himself or herself, restates his or her partner's concern. ("I hear that you feel I've neglected you lately," or "I hear that you may think I need to pitch in more at certain times.")

The presenter then agrees or disagrees that his or her partner has it correct and understands. If the partner doesn't understand, the presenter repeats his or her concern until agreement is reached that the partner "gets it" and understands what's been communicated.

Then, together, they brainstorm the issue, looking for a negotiated solution or a compromise that suits them both and that they both agree to try. If they can't find a solution, at least for now, they agree to disagree, to think about the issue some more, and pick the next time to talk about it.

No one, at any time, defends himself or herself. The point is for the partners to understand and then try to reach a "no-lose" solution they can both live with.

Then they switch positions, following the same steps to try to deal with the other person's concern or issue. (A single issue from each side, each session, is usually enough.)

End the session with something you appreciate about the other person, taking turns, and respond to the appreciation you receive with a simple "thank-you"—not more discussion.

Not all issues can be resolved or settled this way, but for those that can, less resentment will be saved and stored up to use as ammunition during the heat of the next battle. Fewer battles will occur because they will be headed off and dealt with. Even when an issue can't be settled, a sincere attempt goes a long way to bolster love and caring. And sincere appreciation can become a powerful way to express that love.

A Passion for Life

Mates, lovers, and marital partners are not, of course, the only kinds of relationships we need. We also need a circle of friends. Married author Bruce Feiler, for example, was living his passions as a best-selling author and traveler until a cancerous tumor was discovered in his left leg and he was told he might not survive. Faced with that devastating prospect, Feiler turned to a group of six male friends ("men who knew my voice") for their support, advice, and guidance, and to aid in helping his wife raise their twin daughters should he not survive —"to teach them to dream, the joys of travel, and to live life to its fullest"—just as he would have done had he survived. He did survive but ended up losing much of his left leg and chronicling his near-death experience in The Council of Dads: My Daughters, My Illness, and the Men Who Could Be Me (2011).

In an interview with Michel Martin for National Public Radio, Feiler noted, "There have been a lot of studies about happiness, and we know that one of the things that makes people the happiest is close social interaction: lots of friends, being with family, even though that can be problematic." He went on to say, "One of the things that I would say is to sit down with your close friends and tell them what they mean to you. It's incredibly rare, but it can transform all of your lives."

Feiler says he felt robbed and cheated when the diagnosis was pronounced, and he took much of his frustration out on his wife, his family, and his friends, who did their best to understand and tolerate his ever-changing moods. And yet, at the same time, he felt his greatest comfort and support from his family and friends, which led him, even while he thought he might be dying, to consider the idea for a male support group for himself and other men facing death or devastating illness. He called his emerging group a Council of Dads, which later became an organization (Councilofdads.com) to support dying fathers and others who wanted the help of other men in raising and guiding their children. As one result, Feiler is currently writing a book called All Happy Families, based on the love and support he received from his wife and his "family of male friends."

Bruce Feiler clearly felt zero passion for cancer. He hated it. But he had friends and a wife and twin daughters he passionately loved. He had always had a passion for writing and travel. Prior to his diagnosis, he had earned a good living writing over a dozen best-selling books that described his passions for both, including Learning to Bow, the story of a year he spent teaching in rural Japan; Looking for Class, about student life inside Oxford and Cambridge universities; and Under the Big Top, a description of the year he spent performing as a traveling clown in the Clyde Beatty–Cole Bros. Circus.

So what lesson did Feiler extract from facing death and narrowly escaping it? He says that his passion for life, high before, increased even further. His perceptions sharpened. The ordinary now seemed far less ordinary. Most of all, Feiler says he learned the importance of human connections. He realized that he hadn't shared as much as he might have, and as a result, he wasn't as close to others as he now wanted to be. He says that the threat of death waiting on his doorstep deepened his compassion for the suffering of others and that he has applied that understanding to his writing. He says he continues to take the risk of opening up and revealing himself even more to friends and family.

Feiler's experience is a lesson for all of us. As Elbert Hubbard wrote, "A friend is one who knows you and loves you just the same." Feiler raises that notion a step higher: the more a friend knows you, the more he loves you.

Randy has been in and led men's groups since his twenties and can't imagine what his life would have been like without those men, some still very close friends, surrounding him with their wisdom, challenge, comic relief, and real support. He does know what the lives of men who don't have that look like: a lot of isolation or dependency on a partner for meeting all emotional needs and no social safety net like the one that made all the difference to Bruce Feiler.

Another discovery Randy made presenting the Passion Test to both all-male groups and mixed groups is that one of the most powerful ways to get closer to another human being quickly is to learn about and help each other discover and live their passion. In one workshop, a man shared, "Sharing weach other's true passions has been one of the most incredible male bonding experiences of my life!"

Fathers, Sons, Mothers, Daughters

Along with spousal relationships and friendships, the relationships between parents and their children can be full of joy, satisfaction, fulfillment, challenge, and heartache. Most parents want to do right by their children, want the best for them, want them to succeed, and sometimes wish for and provide them with things they themselves did not have growing up.

One of Randy's friends, certified Passion Test facilitator James Garcia, had a stepson whose dream was to become a tennis pro. James tells this story:

When I took the Passion Test facilitator course at the end of January 2012, my stepson Jose was already a valuable member of the men's tennis team at the University of North Carolina. In fact, he was the number-one player for the team. He was a junior studying economics. His dream was to become a professional tennis player.

In mid-February, he called his mother and told her he wanted to finish the year at UNC and then turn pro in June. She was full of concern and worry, thinking that not completing an education was a bad idea. She tried to convince him to finish his studies. Jose had a full scholarship playing for the tennis team, and UNC is one of the top public universities in the country, so his decision to stop attending was not one that a parent could accept all that easily!

Jose was very persistent. Then, not knowing quite what to do, my wife suggested that Jose speak to me and passed me the phone. As I had not only taken the Passion Test but had committed to helping others find their passions, it was crystal clear to me he had to follow his passion, and without any hesitation I told him I would support his plan. He then said, "And what about Mom?" I told him not to worry and that I would take care of that issue. I know that if I had not gotten clear about my own passions and the importance of following one's own dreams, I would have tried to convince him to do the "sensible" thing and finish at UNC.

He followed his heart and put his plan into action. His coaches at UNC were very upset and disappointed to be losing their number-one player. Most of our friends and family members thought we were crazy to support that decision. But because of his great clarity and resolve, Jose was able to find a supportive and generous sponsor from Alabama who just happened to be the father of one of his UNC teammates. He has been playing as a pro for almost three years now, and as of this writing, his ranking is 298 in the Association for Tennis Professionals. We are so proud that he is so committed and successfully living his number-one passion!

Randy recalls a similar story about a mother who was concerned about her daughter's choice of colleges when they were exploring the options together. Mom thought her daughter would be better served by an institution with higher academic standing, but the daughter had discovered a college that had both a social life and a learning environment she felt she could really thrive in. In her heart of hearts, Mom knew that her daughter needed to make her own decision, but she just could not let go of her attachment to the idea that her daughter's success depended on enrolling in the more prestigious institution. During that time, the mom enrolled in the Passion Test facilitator course, and by the end, it not only dawned on her that she could let go of her idea for her daughter, but she began to see how the college her daughter had chosen really was a perfect fit. And it was!

In addition to the couples' Passion Discovery workshop, the Passion Test workshop, and the four-day Passion Test facilitator training course now offered in several countries, there is a Passion Test for Kids and Teens that is especially adapted to young people (ages nine to fourteen) and their families. Time after time, Randy has seen how revolutionary this process can be as a means to reestablish family closeness and the sense that every member of the family is on the same passion team, supporting each other to learn and grow by getting clear about and supporting each other to live their passions.

What we all know is that children learn by example more than what they are told. When parents demonstrate they are committed to living their most passionate lives, the children get the message that they can too. What a difference it would make if all families knew and practiced this.

Passionate Connections

Humans need other humans, even though they come in all shapes and sizes, with all sorts of quirks, hopes, needs, baggage, opinions, dispositions, hopes, and desires. As one of Bruce's clients said, "It's hard enough living alone with me, let alone someone else."

Getting along sometimes means going along. At its best, a relationship based on respect and caring that is bonded by common interests and passions makes getting along and thriving a lot easier. While mutual passions often occur naturally, as part of the natural flow that draws people together, there are also ways to broaden and deepen passions to enhance and strengthen that relationship. You've just read about some pretty good ones here.

CHAPTER 11

Passion for Work

French chef, author, and television personality Eric Ripert said in an interview, "I've had a passion for food ever since I was young. I was always around the kitchen with whoever was cooking, and then—at a very young age—I decided on what they call a 'profession.' I decided to go to culinary school because I had a passion for eating and cooking."

Most people—and certainly a chef—spend more time at work than in any other waking activity. Add commuting time to that and it's not surprising that satisfaction with work has a lot to do with satisfaction with life in general. Yet in a 2013 Gallup Poll, it was found that an astonishing 70 percent of people are not happy with or engaged with the work they do. And though only three out of ten are happy with their work, most people would like to be like Chef Ripert—they would like to feel that passionate about their work. But the sad truth is they don't.

This lack of engagement permeates our modern societies, and even those who are passionate about their work desire a balanced life that includes more beyond work. If you're among the 70 percent of people who aren't happy at work, you might wonder what it looks like to be excited about your workday—and where such inspiration comes from. We'll talk about this in this chapter and give you some specific ideas you can apply to make your work more satisfying.

Early Passions

Emma, a private-practice attorney, was struggling through a difficult period when Bruce saw her in therapy. Emma's mother, who was living with her at the time, was dying of cervical cancer. Emma told him that she was an only child and that she had always been close to her mother, particularly after her parents' divorce.

"I've been in a couple of serious relationships, of course. I'm in one right now," she volunteered, "but I never married and I've always gotten my strength from my mother. She was a lawyer too, who always loved the profession and supported me when I showed an interest. She even let me tag along on some of her court cases while I was growing up. 'A vacation from school,' she called it."

Like her mother, Emma felt passionate about the law. "I guess you could say it's a family tradition now," she said. "But it wasn't my mother who started it. It was mother's father, Grandpa Joe. He wasn't a lawyer, but he was the one who encouraged my mother."

Emma's grandfather grew up and attended high school in a small town a hundred miles east of Minneapolis. After graduation, when he needed a job, he did what was expected—he walked along Main Street, where he spotted a sign in a butcher shop window: "Boy Wanted." He applied and got the job and ended up working as a butcher for the rest of his life. If there had been a "Boy Wanted" sign in the local furniture store or in the window of the only car dealer in town, he would have spent his working life selling furniture or cars.

"I was close to my grandfather," Emma said. "My mother took me to my grandparents' house a lot, and I spent a lot of summers there. Grandpa always said, 'Don't do what I did. Find something you really want to do. Something you love. Like your mother.'"

Emma said her grandfather didn't hate being a butcher but that he felt no particular passion for it, which was why he always encouraged Emma's mother to find her calling and go for it. He then saved what he could to help her through college. After getting her bachelor's degree, her mother earned and borrowed enough to put herself through law school at night.

"It was a long journey," Emma said her mother told her. "But she ended up doing something she loved, and that made the struggle a lot easier."

If you're lucky enough to be aware of your talents and passions early in life, and if you're wise enough to pursue them, then you usually end up in a career you feel passionate about, as Emma and her mother did. They both found what author Shakti Gawain described in her groundbreaking book Creative Visualization (2002): "When you're following your energy and doing what you want, the distinction between work and play dissolves."

Success: Byproduct of Passion

Explorer and botanist Charles Darwin, at the age of twenty, volunteered for a five-year voyage of a lifetime on the H.M.S. Beagle to purse his lifelong passion for collecting and studying plants and animals. It was a trip that changed his own world and radically altered how science viewed itself. That journey ultimately led Darwin to what future scientists called "the best idea anyone ever had"—the notion that all life, both plant and animal, originated from a single source or origin. Darwin was so passionate about this emerging belief that after returning to England, he spent the next thirty-two years studying his collection, drawing inferences, making notes, and finally publishing On the Origin of Species in 1859.

The concept that spawned Darwin's passion ran headlong into the fundamentalist religious beliefs and passions of others, particularly those theologians who argued that man, according to the Gospel, was created by God in His own image in a single stroke on the sixth day, after creating the rest of the world in the first five. Man, these theologians passionately believed, was special and above all the other species.

The two opposing arguments clashed head-to-head in the court case State of Tennessee v. John Thomas Scopes in the summer of 1925, when well-known defense lawyer Clarence Darrow defended ninth-grade science teacher John Scopes's right to teach evolution to his students. William Jennings Bryan, a three-time presidential candidate, argued for Tennessee's right to prohibit such teaching and to require instead the teaching of the Biblical version of man's origin. Despite what most considered a brilliant defense by Darrow, Scopes was found guilty by a jury of his peers—although the Tennessee Supreme Court later overturned that verdict.

Nonetheless, both attorneys, passionate about their professions and about the Scopes case, argued with all the skill and talent they could muster. Both men, like Emma and her mother, loved lawyering. It was not simply how they earned a living, it was a central part of who they felt they were. They cared about the law, thought about it a lot, spent much time in its pursuit, and passionately felt they were doing something of value that added to the community at large. Clarence Darrow once said, "As long as the world shall last, there will be wrongs, and if no man objected and no man rebelled, those wrongs would last forever." He also reportedly said, "I am a friend of the working man, but I would rather be his friend than be one." He didn't consider his work actual work. He did what he loved.

Both Bryan and Darrow were passionate in their pursuit of fairness and justice, as were Mother Teresa and Martin Luther King Jr. in pursuing fairness and justice in their own ways, as were Georgia O'Keeffe and Frederic Remington in the passionate pursuit of their artistic vision of the American West, as was American opera singer Maria Callas in pursing her passion for opera, and as was French physicist Marie Curie—the first woman to win a Nobel Prize in both chemistry and in physics. They all used their talents and gifts to pursue their passion. To succeed, Curie advised, "Believe that you are gifted for something and that that thing must be attained. Discover what you are passionate about and go after it."

All these famous men and women, as well as most others we know and recognize, were both gifted and passionate about what they did, which is a large part of why we know about them—although all would testify that it wasn't fame that drove them. It was doing what they felt passionate about. Passion came first. Success came as a consequence and byproduct.

Passion for Ordinary Folk

Buddha once advised, "Your work is to discover your work and then, with all your heart, give yourself to it." Wouldn't it be great if we all felt that kind of passion for our jobs or professions? The truth is, we all know people who drag themselves out of bed every morning feeling unfulfilled and unhappy, counting the days to retirement. As Lance Secretan observed in his book Inspirational Leadership (1999), "Only a few discover work they truly love." Secretan's observation strikes a familiar chord all too often. As Kenneth Tucker wrote in an online article, "A Passion for Work," "For many people, finding the work they love is a long-surrendered high-school ideal. Instead, each morning they pry themselves out of bed, slip into semi-consciousness, and slug through the day until the last forty-five minutes, when they wait with bated breath for the moment they can leave. Work is what they must do, not what they love to do."

A Native American Passion

One recent graduate from the New Mexico State University nursing program in Las Cruces wrote of her passion for nursing in an online discussion of work passion:

"I am a Native American, a member of the Navajo tribe. My family and I live on the Navajo reservation outside of Ganado, Arizona. During the summer of 2001, prior to the start of my senior year, I had the opportunity to spend four weeks working as a research intern with the University of Texas at Austin Health Promotion & Disease Prevention Research team. It is no exaggeration to say that that experience changed my life.

"The center's mission is to improve the health of underserved populations—such as racial and ethnic minorities, women, people with disabilities, children, adolescents, and the elderly—through research designed to reduce health disparities. Participating in this internship broadened my horizons. It gave me a chance to meet new people, learn to work with computer programs and databases, experience a place different from home, and much more. Most important, my research experience helped me discover a lifelong passion that I never knew I had: to help people and minorities."

One of the secrets of the good life is finding a passion you love and feeding it. That's especially true in the workplace.

Work Satisfaction

A famous polling organization, Harris, reported the following statistics gathered from a survey and interactive study on American job satisfaction in the last decade:

Forty-five percent of workers say they are satisfied with their work—it's "OK"—but that they're not fully engaged.

Thirty-three percent believe they have reached a dead-end in career advancement.

A mere twenty percent say they feel passionate about their jobs.

Amy Tardio, a freelance writer on health and related psychology issues, writes this in an online article entitled "Is the World Ready for a Positive Psychology?": "Imagine that by the year 2051, 50 percent of the American population is feeling fully engaged at work. Government, education, and health care leaders recognize and act on scientific evidence that societies function better when people are doing well. It sounds far-fetched, but then again, ten years ago, so did the notion of a psychology dedicated to the scientific study of positive emotions, strengths, and virtues."

A paltry 50 percent feeling "engaged at work," let alone passionate about it, is still a distressingly low percentage. Even at that, it is a hoped-for number. In the Harris poll cited above, only 20 percent said they felt passionate about their jobs, with a more recent Gallup poll showing a bit better satisfaction—but not a dramatic uptick. How many of the other 80 percent wait for the end of the workday in order to escape their jobs, only to have to get up and go back again the next morning?

It's a sad situation for an individual and a disastrous loss of productivity in the workplace, calculated to be in the billions. In many cases work has become a long social hour where people fill time by chatting with others instead of working. Procrastination, frustration, consternation, and even sabotage of others efforts can take their toll.

So if you're among those who are not passionate about their work and not feeling creative—if you don't feel you're contributing something meaningful or being very productive—how can you find more joy and fulfillment in these days that are ticking away on your life clock, never to be regained?

Passion Strategies for Upping Job Satisfaction

Work sometimes requires a 101-percent attention. You're getting paid to work and expected to perform. But most jobs involve some downtime when you're waiting around for something to happen or doing routine tasks you know well. Your mind inevitably wanders. Since it's wandering anyway, why not point it in a more productive direction? We said "productive"—not shopping for the latest app or gaming before lunch.

Of course, if you're lucky enough to be among the 20 to 30 percent who do feel passionate about their work, you don't need to skirt the routine or the drudgery. But what if you're not? What if you're one of the other 70 to 80 percent? What if you don't hate your work but you don't exactly love it? Then what can you do? Are there ways to make it better? Are there ways to add more passion? What can you do to keep your day job but make it more satisfying to you?

Here are a few suggestions to consider:

1) Try to Wedge Your Passion into Your Work

What if your job is just a job and your primary interest is in the paycheck? Then what do you do? You might start with the assumption that most jobs and workplaces are so complicated that there might be a way to express at least some of your passions within that complicated structure. To do so, of course, you have to know what your passions are or what they could be. Take a look again at the work you did in Chapter 3. Consider those passions you discovered as possibilities within the context of your job, and more importantly, in the context of the overall structure of the company or the organization. And not just the formal structure—the informal as well. Are there opportunities, at least in part, to engage one of your passions within that arena? Is there something for which you could volunteer that would fit one of your passions?

A friend of Bruce's, Shannon, worked as an administrator at an inpatient mental health facility. She decided that she wanted to devote herself to something she felt more passionate about than processing paperwork. One of her passions was travel. After taking a Passion Discovery workshop presented at the facility, she decided to put that passion to work at her workplace. The only problem was, a mental health facility had very little need for travel—especially foreign travel, Shannon's particular passion.

She talked it over with some of the other staff who enjoyed traveling and who appreciated bargains, and they formed an informal travel club that met every first and third Thursday in one of the conference rooms for a brown-bag travel lunch and a discussion of where they might want to go. She put travel posters in her office and started to learn Italian using CDs during her ride to work. Shannon arranged for group rates with a local travel agent, and on one trip to Italy, they paid half the fare of a history professor as payment for him to accompany them and "walk and talk" them through the sights and history of Tuscany. Last I heard, the travel club was still active and Shannon was studying for her travel agent license. Traveling was never part of Shannon's everyday work. She did it on the side during her breaks. She wedged it in and began to think of it not only as a wedge at work but a possible future occupation as well.

One marketing executive who took a Passion Discovery workshop said that when he developed serious health issues, it caused him to rethink his future with his company. His newfound interest in having a healthy workplace inspired him to speak with the company's upper echelon and set up healthy-lifestyle classes for employees to help reduce the company's health insurance costs. He was asked to research what would be required to set up a small workout room with equipment for exercising before and after hours. The company soon benefited, and he was happy to organize and engage in what had become a very personal passion.

Think outside the box to see how you might use one of your passions in your organization. See if you can shape or mold a passion to fit your particular circumstances.

2) Sneak Your Passion into Work

The truth is, no one spends 100 percent of his or her work time working at work. Apple, Inc. is only one company of many that encourages its employees to spend a certain amount of off-time for relaxation, exercise, or visiting with their children in Apple's daycare center. Apple management understands that employees are still churning ideas and creating new concepts while they're relaxing and that after such relaxation, they're refreshed and ready to go again when they return to their desks.

Like everyone, Apple's employees think of other things while at work. Bruce noticed when he worked for a large mental health organization that much of the kibitzing and social life occurred in the coffee room. Discussions lingered far longer than it took to fill a coffee cup, stir in a package of creamer, and drink. Friendships were forged in that room. A few romances and one marriage that he knew of were sparked and kindled while coffee cooled on the counter. He's quite certain that those coffee-room clutches were the best part of the day for at least a few employees.

So the question is, if coffee-room kibitzing is the best part of your workday and you can't figure out a way to make your passion part of your work, is there a way to sneak it in? If nobody works full-time all the time, how can you spend some of your time at work engaging in a passion? When I asked for workshop examples of how that could be done, one self-described news addict said he always carries The New York Times into the office and looks forward to reading it during his lunch hour—especially in the summer, when he carries his paper and his lunch outside, reads on a park bench, and feeds the pigeons. Also, Elmore Leonard, the gritty crime novelist, admitted in a magazine interview that he wrote his first novel during downtime as a car salesman, making notes or writing a page or two when the showroom was empty and there were no "potentials" walking the lot, then hiding them in his desk drawer when customers arrived.

3) Get Clear About Your Work Passions

When Randy shifted toward doing more work in management consulting and organizational psychology, he used a lot of different processes and tools available in the world of organizational management and leadership. After his training as a Passion Test for Business consultant, he became even more passionate about his work with organizations.

One of the first businesses to benefit from Janet Attwood and Chris Attwood's Passion Test for Business employed a thousand workers at inbound call centers in Maine and Mexico. Sales were way down and slipping further. The business was faltering and needed more than a facelift. The owners were initially guided to get clear about their personal passions so they could determine which to apply to help their company get back on its feet and hopefully soar to new levels of productivity and success. They then engaged in a process to discover the unique passions of the company as a whole and how those drove the unique contribution of the company to its sector.

The next phase guided each employee to clarify his or her own work passions and the elements behind them. One employee, Guillermo Nogales, realized he felt passion for working as part of a team, even though he was in a room by himself with a repetitive task. Not a good fit. When he and the owners realized that he needed more contact with fellow employees, he was placed on a team, where he came alive and quickly shot above his sales quota.

Ultimately, some employees were let go and others reassigned to better match their passions within the company and to in turn increase their engagement and productivity. New hires were brought in after having been taken through the

Passion Test for Business, which was a powerful tool that helped achieve a better match between each new hire and the company's passions defined in the first phase of the program.

Knowing your work passions ahead of time can save you a lot of time and frustration when looking for a job or for a slot in a company that better fits who you are, what you're good at, and what you want—that better fits the passions you know of and are clear about.

4) Engage Your Strengths

Nicholas Hall, the manager of the Behavioral Laboratory at Stanford's Graduate School of Business, wrote this in a January 6, 2007 blog titled "Positive Psychology and Person-Job Fit": "Does the new upstart subfield within psychology called positive psychology have anything to add to the domain of people in the workplace? If positive psychology is all about positive emotions and human flourishing, what can it say about our work life and how to be happiest and flourishing in it?" In order to find out, Hall says he "studied the workers themselves."

Following his own passionate interest in the study of occupations and occupational placement, Hall hypothesized that each particular occupation ought to have a unique mix of character strengths that could be measured and quantified using Peterson and Seligman's VIA Signature Strengths Test, which helps individuals understand themselves better and find the most effective way to boost their positive emotions. After studying hundreds of individuals in different occupations, his results demonstrated that success in each particular occupation showed a unique profile of character strengths. Artists, for example, scored high on appreciation of beauty and excellence, while lawyers were found to be high on analytic skills but generally low in spirituality strengths. From his results, Hall concluded that a key to job success and satisfaction is finding a job or career that fits an individual's character strengths and that allows him or her to develop and express passions that naturally spring from those strengths.

Peterson and Seligman's VIA Signature Strengths Test (free with a printout interpretation at www.authentichappiness.org) identifies an individual's five top "signature character strengths" from a possible list of twenty-four. Those strengths are called signature strengths because, like your handwritten signature, the pattern is unique to each individual. The research clearly shows that a workplace that encourages and rewards employees for using their character strengths has less turnover, higher employee satisfaction, and greater productivity, which ultimately leads to higher profitability.

In his book, The Happiness Hypothesis (2006), University of Virginia psychology professor Jonathan Haidt writes, "Knowing your strengths and weaknesses may give you insight into why some parts of your job are enjoyable while others fill you with dread. If you have the luxury of adjusting the scope of your job, then of course you should focus on the tasks that draw on your strengths while delegating away the parts that don't, even if you are perfectly competent at them."

Even if others define your job, you still may have some latitude over how you approach the job. If two of your top strengths are curiosity and a love of learning, for example, you might give yourself the challenge of learning something new on the job each week. That will at least give you something to look forward to and may lead to opportunities of which you aren't aware. If one of your top strengths is appreciation of beauty and excellence, there may be ways to "stop and smell the roses" more often at work, whatever those roses might be. Haidt advises that the roses at work could "include the people you serve or work with." He goes on to say, "Identify areas of excellence in other people and then tell them what you've noticed. When your strengths help you build relationships, the payoff is most likely to be long lasting."

The online VIA Signature Strengths Survey takes about forty-five minutes to complete. With those results and a printout in hand, you can begin to figure out how to look for opportunities to engage one or more of your top character strengths—not only at work, but in other areas of life.

5) Seek Balance

Many of today's jobs require what we call blurred hours. They blur standard work hours and personal time with a continuous flurry of e-mails, online searches, and smartphone pings in the middle of the night. With organizations going global, related businesses demand instant information around the clock. One woman I know sleeps with her smartphone next to her pillow and wakes up with every ping. "It's usually a junk message," she rationalizes. "But you never know."

Not surprisingly, research undertaken at the Center for Work-Life Policy, a New York think tank, indicates that 45 percent of managers who work for global corporations spend a minimum of sixty-plus hours a week on the job and that they are constantly revising schedules, adjusting to constantly changing demands, and answering e-mails that "breed like rabbits."

In her book Falling in Love with Work: A Practical Guide to Igniting Your Passion for Your Career (2011), Denice

Kronau, a former corporate CEO, describes a life and schedule that often flew her over enough time zones to glaze her eyes and spin her sensibilities. She says she once spent a cramped sixteen hours in the air from New York to New Delhi to attend a one-hour meeting and then turned around and flew home on the next flight, all of which she says finally drove her "beyond exhaustion." She writes that "the rules are changing and more and more of us are working longer hours, giving up weekends, taking on impossible deadlines, and doing work we hate, often because we fear downsizing and being laid off."

When you're exhausted, worn out, or frightened, engaging a passion sinks to the bottom of your priority list. All you want to do is escape or sleep. Denice Kronau finally took time off to sit and relax on a beach in Nantucket, where she immediately concluded that work was important, but not that important—it was not everything.

As stress management expert Dr. Kathleen Hall says in her talks to business managers, "We have overstretched our personal boundaries and forgotten that true happiness comes from living an authentic life fueled with a sense of purpose and balance."

6) Maintain a Grateful Attitude

In telling her story in the online article "Not a Job, a Passion," Michelle Tranchina writes that she had always wanted to work in the health care field while growing up, but after graduating from college, she ended up in hotel management, a job she found routine and uninspiring. After rethinking her options, she enrolled in massage therapy school at night and eventually started seeing customers in her home until she was able to open a small clinic and make enough to quit her day job. "By following my instinct," she writes, "I wake up every day excited to go to work. It's not a job. It's my life. I'm very passionate about my new career. I see myself doing this well into old age." She is grateful for a job that finally allows her to live her passion, but she adds that she was also grateful for her hotel management work because the hours were flexible and the money provided her the opportunity to return to school to follow that passion.

In working with his coaching clients on work and career satisfaction, Randy never suggests that his clients leave their day job if their passion is gone. Instead, he helps clients to get clear about their passions and then note what elements or larger mission in their current job truly fulfills them. Sometimes a reframing of that kind can lead to insight that puts the client in a better place to make decisions about whether to stay in a career or move on.

Passion and Job Success

In one study of working adults, Christopher Peterson found that the character trait of zest, which he defined as "vitality and passion," was highly associated with "viewing one's work as a 'calling' and a source of fulfillment that is socially useful and personally meaningful, rather than as financial reward or career advancement."

Howard Thurman—author, philosopher, educator, theologian, and civil rights leader—once said in a speech to college graduates, "Don't ask yourself what the world needs. Ask yourself what makes you come alive. Then go and do that. Because what the world needs are people who have come alive." In relating that notion to work, psychologist Jonathan Haidt advises, "Go out of your way to become more involved in an organization to which you already belong. Do something because you want to do it, not because you have to do it."

Best Possible Job Ratings

Think a minute about the qualities and attributes you would ideally like to have in your job or career and see if they match what you actually find.

Instructions: Of the ten work qualities listed below, rank them in order from 1 to 10, with 1 being the most important and 10 the least. Start with the most and the least important—with numbers 1 and 10—and then work back toward the middle.

JOB FACTOR	RANK
1. Ability to do the job my own way	
2. Easy commute or no commute	
3. Challenging tasks	
4. Getting along with coworkers	
5. Fulfilling work	
6. Good health and retirement benefits	
7. Good pay	
8. Stability and security	
9. Task variety	
10. Flexible hours	

11. Work that is my calling	
12. I usually look forward to going to work	

PRACTICAL JOB SCORE
(Sum of rank numbers for items 2, 5, 7, 8, 9, and 11) [ ]

PASSION JOB SCORE
(Sum of rank numbers for items 1, 3, 4, 6, 10, and 12) [ ]

The LOWER the total practical job score and the LOWER the passion job score, the HIGHER your score in that category because lower numbers mean higher rankings. Your scores show the relative importance (for you) of practicality versus meaning/passion for work. Your scores and rankings may change from time to time, depending on your changing priorities and life circumstances.

Steve Jobs on Start-up Passion

When Steve Jobs was asked at a conference what advice he could offer a small, start-up company, he said, "Building a business and making money is hard sometimes. There are insurmountable barriers that require perseverance to overcome. If you're not passionate about what you're doing, you'll simply quit and move on to something a little more appealing, failing to achieve the success you seek." That's excellent counsel whether you're starting a small company or simply working for a company. It's passion for the job that makes the job worthwhile.

PART III: Sustaining Your Passions

"Passion and satisfaction go hand in hand, and without them, any happiness is only temporary because there's nothing to make it last."

Nicholas Sparks

CHAPTER 12

Savoring

Passing through life is not quite the same as savoring life's experience. Skimming the surface, staying afloat, and paddling around obstacles is not quite the same as diving in and exploring beneath the surface. When reading a book, George Herbert, the sixteenth-century Welsh poet, advised to do more than simply read: "Read as you taste fruit or savor wine, or enjoy friendship, love or life." Motivational speaker Wayne Dyer put it this way, "Develop an appreciation for the present moment. Seize every second of your life and savor it. Value your present moments. Using them up in any self-defeating ways means you've lost them forever."

Consider a mind experiment. Think again about one of your current or potential passions and then visualize yourself engaged in that passion. Imagine that scene as vividly as you can. See yourself actually there. Hear the sounds or the silence that surrounds you. Taste, sense, feel, and savor all the sensations and the pleasant feelings that accompany them.

Randy sometimes deliberately directs his attention to the simple things in life that we can easily forget to savor: a hot shower, the first sip of one's favorite brew, a friend's laughter, the slow drift of a leaf falling off a tree, or one of many spectacular sunrises and sunsets that pull him to his window or out the door of his Santa Fe home. He confesses to being a "connoisseur of clouds." Much of the pleasure in life comes from savoring those moments, especially when they involve one of our passions. A major motivation for sustaining our passions is the joy and the pleasure we experience while savoring them.

All good advice, but how exactly do you fully savor each passing moment? That's what this chapter is all about.

Learning How to Savor

We can learn a lot about what it looks like to savor your passion from one fifty-something marina owner named Logan who said he signed up for a Passion Discovery workshop on a whim. "Hers, not mine," he added. "My wife insisted." Logan said he had done so well building up his business over the years that he was now able to turn the day-to-day operations over to one of his employees and take life a little easier. He said he wanted to spend more time sitting out on his deck under an old shade tree, watching the boats float by on the Miles River, and then enjoying a good evening meal. The problem was, after arranging his semiretirement, his wife, who had joined him in the Passion Discovery workshop, accused him of "invading" her territory. As it turned out, he wanted to do a little more than simply enjoy a dinner out on his deck. He wanted to cook dinner—formerly the exclusive domain of his wife. Now, according to her, he planned to "take over." Her mission at the workshop, it seems, was to find him another way to spend his newfound time that would keep him out of "her" kitchen.

After completing one of the Passion Discovery exercises, Logan said he wasn't surprised that cooking topped his list of potential passions. He said he had always loved a good meal and thought that preparing one would add to that pleasure. He was an avid fan of the Food Channel cooking shows, especially the male chefs like Emeril John Lagasse and Alton Brown. "I'll admit," he confessed at the workshop, "cooking is my wife's area. It's her kitchen—but I've seen some mighty good meals on these shows."

Logan's wife, Ellie, agreed that cooking was not necessarily one of her passions. She had others though. Reading floated up on her list of possibilities. "I used to read a lot," she said. "I always get swept away in a good story, especially a biography. I just haven't read much lately. I haven't had the time."

After negotiating a compromise, they agreed that Logan would cook Wednesday evening dinners—if he learned to cook "something edible"—which freed up Wednesday afternoons for Ellie to spend browsing book reviews online or savoring a biography for the pure pleasure of it.

Besides cooking a meal at home, Logan struck a deal with one of the caterers who served the yachts at the marina. He arranged to work gratis as a prep chef on Thursday mornings during the high season. He would learn food-prep basics and then bring home a full meal from what they'd prepared that day. As Logan's wife found more time on her hands, she started a book club and became a judge for the local high school writing contest.

What started out as a tense situation for Logan and his wife ended with many happy moments savoring gourmet meals together and discussing the latest best sellers. "The kitchen is his anytime he wants it. I'm not finding much time to cook these days," his wife announced at our last workshop meeting.

Savoring the Past, Present, and Future

Psychologist Fred Bryant describes what he calls three temporal forms of savoring: (1) anticipatory, (2) in-the-moment, and (3) reminiscent. Not only do we savor experiences as they occur, we savor them beforehand as we think about and plan for future events, and then we savor them again as we think back and fondly recall them. Logan, for example, savored recipes as he thumbed through magazines and books in anticipation of preparing a meal. "My mouth waters just looking at some of those pictures," he volunteered in the workshop.

He savored Wednesday night dinners as he anticipated making them, as he prepared and ate them, and then again the next day as he looked back and thought about how much he enjoyed preparing and serving them. The more skills he developed, the more he savored and the more pleasure he derived from his newly engaged passion. He savored cooking in all three of Bryant's temporal forms—anticipatory, in-the-moment, and reminiscent.

Ellie, after reinstituting her former passion for reading, found herself more often pausing to read more carefully, trying to catch every nuance of the author's meaning. Upon finishing a book, she would anticipate reading another by the same author or on the same subject. She often recalled a piece of information that she had found interesting. She looked forward to book club meetings where she could share her thoughts and learn how others had experienced the same book.

After practicing savoring in a Passion Discovery workshop, she paused more often to savor an especially beautiful passage and consider what it was for her that made that passage so beautiful. "It's like holding a bite of chocolate in your mouth a little longer," she said, "and letting the taste linger on the tongue." She anticipated reading, savored as she read, and then savored again as she thought about the book afterward.

Bryant, who has researched and studied savoring more than anyone, says that we extract less from all three forms of savoring than we could. His research demonstrates that by deliberately practicing savoring, by slowing down and focusing more often—especially before, during, and after experiencing a passion activity—we can significantly increase the depth, quality, and enjoyment of the experience.

Testing Your Ability to Savor

Some people naturally savor their experiences more than others—that is, they linger longer and pay more attention to the sensual or reflective quality of life in the course of an ordinary day. The following test will give you a general idea of how much you tend to savor past, present, and future events or experiences, and how you might more often use a variety of occasions to squeeze a little more juice from life. After you practice the act of savoring a while, you might rate yourself again to see how far you've come.

Instructions: Rate yourself on how much you agree with the following statements, using the scale below:

Don't Agree		Mostly Agree		Strongly Agree		
1	2	3	4	5	6	7

1. I often enjoy looking ahead as much as being there.

   1 2 3 4 5 6 7

2. I enjoy planning and anticipating future events.

   1 2 3 4 5 6 7

3. I get excited before an exciting event occurs.
   1 2 3 4 5 6 7

4. It's easy for me to imagine good times ahead.
   1 2 3 4 5 6 7

5. Anticipation is part of the joy of doing.
   1 2 3 4 5 6 7

Add your scores for
Anticipatory Savoring [ ]

Low Savoring > 5 - 11
Medium Savoring > 12 - 18
High Savoring > 19 - 25

Again, rate yourself on how much you agree with the following statements, using the same scale as before:

Don't Agree		Mostly Agree		Strongly Agree		
1	2	3	4	5	6	7

1. When I find something I like, I slow down and savor it.
   1 2 3 4 5 6 7

2. It's like me to stop the car or stop walking and look around when I see something of beauty.
   1 2 3 4 5 6 7

3. It's usually easy for me to hold on to a good feeling.
1 2 3 4 5 6 7

4. I know how to prolong enjoyment.
1 2 3 4 5 6 7

I know how to fully appreciate good times.
1 2 3 4 5 6 7

Add your scores for
Immediate Savoring =

Low Savoring > 5 – 11
Medium Savoring > 12 – 18
High Savoring > 19 – 25

Finally, rate yourself on how much you agree with the following statements, using the same scale as before:

Don't Agree		Mostly Agree		Strongly Agree		
1	2	3	4	5	6	7

1. Looking back at good things often brings me good feelings.
1 2 3 4 5 6 7

2. I like to savor the small things in life.
1 2 3 4 5 6 7

3. Reminiscing rekindles the good feelings I once had.
1 2 3 4 5 6 7

4. I enjoy recalling and sharing good things that have happened to me.

1 2 3 4 5 6 7

5. I like to remember good times just to savor them.

1 2 3 4 5 6 7

Add your scores for Reminiscent Savoring ☐

Low Savoring > 5 - 11
Medium Savoring > 12 - 18
High Savoring > 19 - 25

Externalizer or Internalizer?

Another dimension of savoring is whether you are what psychologists call an internalizer or an externalizer—that is, whether you lean more toward or prefer an internal mental life or an external experience.

The earliest work on measuring the difference between internalizers and externalizers was done in relative secret by psychologist John Gittinger, working for the Central Intelligence Agency in the late fifties through the sixties. Gittinger and the Agency were interested in developing a personality evaluation method that would determine both the strengths and vulnerabilities of employees, agents, interrogators, and others. They were partly looking for how to "get to someone" by determining which side of the brain to appeal to and which side to exploit.

Gittinger developed what he called a Personality

Assessment System (PAS). One of his primary PAS dimensions was internalizer/externalizer. Gittinger defined an internalizer as someone with an ability and inclination to "manipulate internal stimuli or symbols without being distracted by the external world." An externalizer, on the contrary, is someone who is "more dependent on input from the outside" in making decisions. Internalizers, for example, tend to do better on certain subscales of standard intelligence tests, especially those that require more thinking than visualization. Externalizers fare better when the tasks involve visual matching.

The PAS has been continually revised and updated since those early days and is used for many other purposes—education and career development among them—and the distinction between externalizers and internalizers has remained robust and useful, as you'll see below.

The externalizer/internalizer dimension is a continuum, with most people falling somewhere between the two extremes—although even those in the middle tend to lean more in one direction or the other. When it comes to savoring experience, it's helpful to know which way you lean so that you can favor your natural assets and, at the same time, improve those that you're not naturally good at.

Instructions: Rate yourself on how much you agree with the following statements, using the scale below:

Don't Agree		Mostly Agree		Strongly Agree		
1	2	3	4	5	6	7

1. Sometimes I get so lost in thought that I lose track of what's going on around me.

1 2 3 4 5 6 7

2. My imagination is quite active.

1 2 3 4 5 6 7

3. I am a thinker who frequently examines my own behavior.

1 2 3 4 5 6 7

4. It's easy for me to imagine good times ahead.

1 2 3 4 5 6 7

5. I am better at solving problems abstractly by just thinking about them in my head.

1 2 3 4 5 6 7

Add your scores for Internalizer [ ]

Low Internalizer > 5 – 11
Medium Internalizer > 12 – 18
High Internalizer > 19 – 25

Again, rate yourself on how much you agree with the following statements:

Don't Agree		Mostly Agree			Strongly Agree	
1	2	3	4	5	6	7

1. If something is happening around me, it draws my attention.

1 2 3 4 5 6 7

2. I get bored easily if nothing is happening.

1 2 3 4 5 6 7

3. I am more interested in doing than thinking.

1 2 3 4 5 6 7

4. I tend to notice small changes in the environment.

1 2 3 4 5 6 7

5. I am more comfortable solving a problem I can physically grasp than something I have to think about abstractly.

1 2 3 4 5 6 7

Add your scores for Externalizer ☐

Low Externalizer > 5 – 11
Medium Externalizer > 12 – 18
High Externalizer > 19 – 25

The important question is not whether you are an internalizer or an externalizer but how to make the best of whichever you are and improve what you don't usually tend to do that could be of benefit. If you tend to be an internalizer, that means intentionally instructing yourself, at least on occasion, to get out of your head and pay full sensual attention to what your eyes, ears, and nose are telling you. If you tend to be an externalizer, it means getting into your head once in a while and deliberately savoring memories of past events and pleasant thoughts of the future. If you are balanced, it means choosing when to move from one mode to the other so that you get the most from each.

Savoring as You Go Along

There is a saying in the Zen tradition: "No day comes twice. Every moment savored is more precious than jade." In a restaurant review for the Santa Monica Daily Press, reviewer Merv Hecht wrote, "It's not the same old Drago it once was. Like most high-end restaurants, it changes from time to time. And when I was last there, I found a number of changes on the menu and in the staff. That's one of the problems with writing a review suggesting that one restaurant is the best in any way. The number of replies from readers goes way up. Everyone has his or her own opinion of what's best. But the bigger problem is that in the restaurant business, things change so often. Nothing stays the best forever." The title of Hecht's article is "Nothing Lasts Forever." If menus, chefs, and restaurants don't last forever, what does?

Bruce shares a pizza anecdote, and perhaps an antidote as well:

When I have a favorite restaurant, or a favorite anything, I don't want it to change or move away. When my daughter was five and I drove her through my old neighborhood, I remember slowing down and pronouncing my disappointment at the disappearance of my favorite after-school haunt—the Harford Road Pizza Palace. "Dad," she rolled her eyes and said, "how long has it been since you had a pizza there?"

"I don't care," I told her, slowing down as I drove along the block, hoping I had forgotten the exact location. I didn't want them to close down or go anywhere. When I want a Pizza Palace pizza, I want them to be there.

The older I get, the more aware I am that pizza palaces have a lifespan—they suddenly appear, they change, they disappear—and I'm increasingly aware of three related concepts. First, everything changes. Second, I change. Third, my time on earth is limited. A psychologist friend and early mentor of mine, Don Nachand, once told me on one of our evening strolls along the beach in front of the mental hospital where I began my career, "If everyone bought their coffin in their mid-twenties and sat it in their living room, they'd appreciate life a little more as they went along." That advice always reminds me to savor the pizza in front of me—this could be the last chance I'll have to eat that or any other pizza.

Savoring the Horizon

When participants in one Passion Discovery workshop went around the room to say why they had signed up, a thirty-six-year-old interior designer said, "I guess I don't want to limit myself to who I am right now. I want to expand my horizons. I want to be more." She said she remembered when she was twelve and first realized that death was real and that people she knew—her parents, her grandparents—would actually die. It occurred to her at the time that it could even happen to her, although that day was still so far off it wasn't worth considering. Now she said she looked at death a little differently. "With well over a third of life behind me," she said, "I realize how short it is. One of the reasons I'm here is to get as much as out of the rest of it as I can."

"That's a depressing thought," another workshop member spoke up and said. "I don't even like to think about dying."

Another class member injected, "I wouldn't call the thought of death depressing. I'd call it bittersweet. The bitter part is knowing we won't be around forever, but that fact always reminds me to savor the sweet part while I'm still here."

As the workshop leader, Bruce couldn't have said it any better. That bittersweet notion fits in perfectly with the accumulating psychological research that shows that remembering that life is fleeting oddly reduces stress ("This too will end. Why worry about it?") and that at the same time, the awareness of death heightens appreciation of life. Remembering that he will never again have another Pizza Palace pizza reminds him to slow down and savor what's in front of him right now, at this moment in life. And as all parents know, it's important to savor each stage of a child's growth before it merges into the next—and then they're gone.

Seeing, Tasting, Smelling, Hearing, and Touching

As we grow older, our senses gradually lose their sensitivity. The corneas of our eyes become less transparent, the pupils grow smaller, the lenses harden and alter in ways that make focusing more difficult, and our field of vision gradually shrinks. Hearing loss starts in middle age as the eardrum slowly tightens and loses it elasticity. The 245 taste buds that coat the tongue at the age of thirty slowly diminish to a mere 90 by the age of seventy. A hot New Mexico chili pepper that burns the tongue at age six is mild at fifty-six. Smell is most acute between the ages of twenty and forty, before it begins its slow decline. The loss of skin tissue and muscle elasticity gradually decreases our sensitivity to touch.

But worse than the loss of our sensory acuity, we get so

busy in our harried lives that we lose interest in sensing and savoring. What we couldn't wait to see, feel, touch, smell, and taste at age five, we ignore at age fifty-five. Just when we need to sharpen our sensory perception, our agendas and other priorities distract us.

In one Passion Discovery workshop exercise, Bruce asked each participant to select an orange from a basket. "But don't just pick any orange," he told them. "Be selective. Pick the one that seems to want to be picked." The idea, Bruce told them, was to get to know a specific orange—to sensually know it—its size, its particular shape, its dimpled texture, its smell, the coolness of its skin as they ran their fingertips across its surface, and the feel of slight moisture on it and on their cheeks as they traced it across their face. After a minute or so, they'd all discuss the sensual elements inherent in their particular orange and how their orange was different from all the others. Bruce told them they wouldn't forget this orange for a while because they had intently savored it. He invited them to take their orange home and get to know it even better—the resistance of the outer layer as they cut the orange in half, the shape and arrangement of the half-cut seeds, the aroma that immediately escapes and intensifies as they bring their nose closer, the sound of the juice as it dribbles into a glass, and finally, the taste of the juice as they swish it around in their mouth and feel it wash down their throat.

"I found it a little like a wine tasting," one participant volunteered in the following week's class, "where you hold the glass up to the light and examine the color, then sniff it before you taste it by swishing it around on your tongue."

Randy recalls a similar experience: "A large group of us gathered on a hillside with a gentle monk in the spring sunshine, each of us having been given an apple and instructed not to eat it, at least not right away. For a half hour, we were taken on a guided visualization journey with our apple—how our particular apple had begun its journey on a tree, and all the people, places, and adventures it had encountered all the way from that tree to reach the palm of each of our hands. By the time we finally took our first bite, it was unlike any other apple we had ever tasted. It was our apple. We knew that apple. We appreciated it. We tasted its flavor. We savored its flavor in the moment, and the sensations lingered.

"Later that afternoon, following the monk down a hillside trail, Randy recalls how the simple act of walking had a similar profound and delightful effect when fully attended to and savored."

Full Absorption

It's easy to recall how our senses were keener as children—how much more aware we were of the taste, smell, and feel of objects. It's amazing how much of that childlike sensitivity we can recover simply by paying closer attention to experiences as we move through them.

Joan and Rona, gay social workers who took a Passion Discovery workshop together, were already well aware of how they injected passion and savoring into their lives. They both worked for the Child Protective Division of the county Social Services Department, a demanding job that was often heartbreaking. Joan had grown up in what she called the hill country of Western Pennsylvania, forty miles south of Pittsburgh. She said she had always loved roaming the hills nearby, and she missed them after accepting a job in the flat marshland of Maryland's Eastern Shore.

After Joan met Rona, she took Rona back to Western

Pennsylvania to give her a feel for the place. After returning several times, Rona fell in love with the hill country too. They decided to save for a small cabin where they could spend three-day weekends and summer vacations.

"It's our escape," Rona told the Passion Discovery class. "We walk the backwoods trails and feel the change of seasons in our bones. There's a creek we cross, where we sometimes take off our shoes and socks and just sit on a rock and let that cool water trickle through our toes."

That's the kind of fully savored experience we more often find on vacation when we round a corner and are suddenly confronted by a soaring mountain, a sparkling lake, or a pristine meadow in full bloom. New and beautiful vistas more often draw us in and awaken our senses than does the beauty around us every day. The question is, how can we more often fully absorb and savor the day-to-day beauty when we've seen it many times before and have come to take it for granted? We need to find out how to more often remember and live Harada Sekkei Roshi's advice in The Essence of Zen (1998): "A hundred flowers blossom in spring, the moon shines in autumn, there is a fresh breeze in summer, and there is snow in winter. If your mind isn't occupied with trivial matters, every time is a good time to enjoy the beauty around you."

Drawing on Life

Bruce shares another process that facilitates savoring: "One exercise I sometimes offer in a Passion Discovery class is what I call the Internal Camera exercise. I got the idea from a woman who took my first Passion Discovery workshop. After completing her Past Memories exercise, she said she recalled enrolling in a sketching class as an elective while a freshman in college. For one assignment, she was instructed to find an interesting object—something outdoors—then sketch it in detail and bring the drawing to class.

She said she drove around town until she spotted the rusting roof of an old abandoned 1940s Pontiac coupe poking up above a metal fence. She got permission from the owner to sit her stool down and sketch "that beautiful old hulk." She said she has never forgotten those details—how the curve of the roof sloped down to meet the hood and then curved down again as it flowed toward the fender. She said she could vividly see that car again as she described it in class—the pop-out wheel guards, that laughing teeth-like grill, and the bullet—Pontiac's hood ornament that looked like it could rip someone open if the car had lowered its hood and charged. The image forged an indelible impression in her memory. "I was studying it minutely," she said, "and then had to reproduce it. I couldn't erase that picture from my mind if I tried." Oddly, or perhaps not so oddly, she even recalled the angle of the sun across the yard that day and the colors of the owner's plaid shirt.

When I started retelling that story to participants in other Passion Discovery classes, I followed it with a lunch-break assignment. I allowed an additional fifteen minutes for workshop participants to find their own "interesting object," either inside or outside the building, and then study it intently from every angle so they could describe it in such a way that everyone else could see it in their mind's eye when it was described to them. During the midafternoon break, I asked them to revisit their object and listen for any sounds that surrounded it, touch and feel it, and then notice how the light and shadows upon it may have changed since their first visit.

The point of the exercise, of course, was to reinforce that

childlike savoring that we all tend to lose somewhere along the way and partially regenerate it with practice. By deliberately stopping and savoring an experience or an object, particularly when engaged in one of your passions, your perceptions will immediately brighten in a way that creates unforgettable times and memories.

Building a Memory Bank

By recalling events and objects you savored in the past, you re-experience the good feelings that accompanied them. You may often thumb through an old photo album or view a slide show for the purpose of recalling and savoring those memories, many of which you may have forgotten, at least in detail, without those photographic memory joggers. Thousands—perhaps millions—of pleasant times are stored in your memory banks, many slumbering in a back corner until the light of memory is shined on them. The question is, how can you access and savor those experiences and memories more often? How can you shine a light upon them?

One way is to keep a running list of memories as they spontaneously come to mind. Write down a brief description or some key words to help you remember. As your list of memories grows, examine it every once in a while by selecting a memory that's meaningful in some way and then savoring it. Relive it in your mind's eye. Recall how you felt at the time, or if you can't recall the feelings, imagine how you would have felt. In a short time you'll be surprised—perhaps even amazed—at the number of pleasant memories you'll recall in detail and how deliberately savoring one every so often can lift your mood and spirits.

If you're keeping a gratitude journal and taking the time

to savor daily entries, one way to add to your pleasant-memory bank is to take an extra minute to recall a particular time, age, or stage of your life and think of the pleasant events or occurrences that happened during that time. Then add that to your journal. As William Marshall once said, "I wish life had a remote. Play the easy times. Pause the good times. Fast-forward the bullshit. Rewind the memories."

Sharing Your Memories

Another way to enhance savoring is to share pleasant memories with someone you love or care for. One exercise Bruce sometimes recommends for couples is what he calls Pleasant Moment Tracking. Each partner is asked to start paying attention to three or four tiny pleasant moments that usually slip beneath the radar during the day. In the evening—maybe before bed, in the quiet time before they turn in—they are to share those pleasant times with their partner and explain why they felt so good about them. It's an exercise in heightened appreciation and better understanding themselves and each other.

Here are a few shared examples heard from these couples over the years:

Walking tall when I went out to get the mail. My muscles felt great. It was good to be alive.

The taste of mint toothpaste on my tongue this morning. I don't usually pay attention to that. I'm always thinking about what's coming up during the day ahead.

Bo, my dog, leaping up and greeting me at the door as soon as I opened it.

The wind curling around the back of my neck with the car window open.

The smell of fresh coffee drifting through a coffee shop door.

Watching a flag wave and feeling very patriotic.

Randy and Karin have adopted a practice they call their Five Minute Journal. At the end of the day, they each take five minutes to jot down what they are grateful for and one thing they appreciate about the other person. They each take about thirty seconds to share what they quickly wrote down. Sometimes they make it an early-morning ritual. Over coffee they write down something they think would make the day great for them and something they appreciate about each other. They've found that this simple exercise helps them to savor their everyday life experience and feel closer to each other at the same time. You can find out more about the Five Minute Journal at Fiveminutejournal.com.

***

Savoring, like any other habit, builds on itself. As your passions grow, you increasingly find more times and moments worth savoring—past, present, and anticipatory future—and in turn, your passions expand. Like a continually filling treasure chest, you end up with plenty to choose from and savor each time you open it.

Chapter 13

Being in Flow

Nearly twenty years ago, Mihaly Csikszentmihalyi—Mike from Chapter 2—developed a concept of flow that burst onto the positive psychology scene with an immediate and widespread impact. Flow is defined as a psychological state in which you are so absorbed in an activity that you and the activity seamlessly "flow together." Mike describes flow this way:

Being so completely involved in an activity for its own sake that the ego falls away. Time flies. Every action, movement, and thought follows inevitably from the previous one, like playing jazz. Your whole being is involved, and you're using your skills to the utmost. It is completely focused motivation. It is a single-minded immersion and represents perhaps the ultimate in harnessing the emotions in the service of performing and learning.

In flow, the emotions are not just contained and channeled, but positive, energized, and aligned with the task at hand. To be caught in the ennui of depression or the agitation of anxiety is to be barred from flow. The hallmark of flow is a feeling of spontaneous joy, even rapture, while performing a task (Csikszentmihalyi and Nakamura, 2005).

Passion and flow are intimately connected. When you are in flow, you experience more passion. The more passion you experience, the more flow naturally runs through you. In this chapter, we explore the eight elements of flow. We'll also give you the chance to assess your own ability to flow in an exercise at the end of the chapter.

The Elements of Flow

The two fathers of positive psychology—Martin Seligman and Mihaly Csikszentmihalyi, the Marti and Mike we introduced in Chapter 2—met early in their careers. Marti may have saved Mike's life one evening when they were both attending a psychology convention on the big island of Hawaii. Just as the sun started to set, Mike, an excellent swimmer, ventured out from shore to get a little exercise when a backwash swept him out farther than he had intended to go. The harder he swam, the farther from shore he got. As he tells the story, he was prepared to die when an incoming wave suddenly caught him from beneath and swept him onto the beach. Marti, who happened to be walking along that deserted shore to get his own exercise that evening, found Mike in the sand semiconscious, and he immediately summoned help. The two have been best friends and collaborators ever since.

Much of Mike's passion for positive psychology emanates from his experience as a child in World War II. Born in Italy, he spent a short time during the war in a German prison camp, where he played chess to divert his attention from the tragedy and inhumanity that surrounded him. After the war, by the age of twenty-two, he had emigrated to the United States to study psychology at the University of Chicago, where he eventually earned his PhD and then taught. Throughout his early college years, he never forgot how playing chess helped pass away those long hours in the camp and how the challenge of playing against older, more experienced players forced him to focus so intently that he often lost track of time.

He also related how a few artists he came to know in

Chicago—all of whom were intently and passionately involved with their art—experienced that same sense of focused concentration and losing a sense of time. Several described "forgetting themselves" as their art and their effort seemed to "flow together," with no sense of time passing. Fascinated by what he heard, Mike decided to undertake a formal study of what he came to call the flow experience, at first studying a larger group of artists and then expanding his research to educators and others who identified themselves as highly involved and passionate about what they did. After studying flow in hundreds of individuals and in a large number of diverse groups, Mike identified eight elements common to flow. Each of these is described below, along with comments from those whose experiences match the element:

1) The activity is "autotelic," or an end in itself, done for its own sake.

Flow activities are engaged in for their pure joy and pleasure—for an internal reward rather than for money, praise, prestige, advancement, or any other external return, even though an external reward may result. People who engage in flow activities say things like the following:

"I'm a damn good trial lawyer. Just don't tell anyone, especially my husband. If they didn't pay me to do this, I'd do it anyway."

"Ever since I got the least bit good at the piano, I can sit and play for hours and enjoy every minute of it."

"Every chance I get, I take out a model airplane and work on it. It relaxes me. There is nothing I like doing better."

2) The immediate goal is clear every step of the way.

In most activities, you sort of know what you're doing but aren't 100 percent focused on precisely what comes next, step-by-step. In flow, the next step is immediate, precise, and clear. You know exactly what to do next and what to do after that. This aspect of flow is illustrated by the following comments:

"When I play Bach's Prelude in C Major, the music sheet's right there in front of me. All I have to do is place my fingers where the notes tell me to place them and then keep moving my fingers as my eyes run across the page."

"I till three rows to prepare for vegetable planting every year. It's always a feeling of accomplishment, like I'm making progress, when I turn that tiller around and start up the next row and then turn around again and head down the next."

"When I have a chapter to read for class, I set a goal of ten pages. When I've finished that, I might read more, but I know exactly what I've done and where I have to go from there."

3) You get instant feedback.

When you're in flow, the immediate feedback you get shows you exactly how you're doing as you go along. Some people who experience instant feedback describe it as follows:

"When I feed my birds in the morning, I know immediately if they're happy or sad. If they're happy, they chirp like crazy and hop from perch to perch. If they're not feeling well, they just sit there."

"The catcher signals an outside curve. I grind the ball in my glove, then wind up and let it fly. If I hit or miss that spot, I see it right away and the catcher tells me with his glare."

4) There is an even balance between challenge and skill.

An activity that is too easy is no challenge. It's boring. An activity that's too hard, one that's beyond your skill level, is frustrating and anxiety producing. Flow runs down the middle: the challenge is neither too easy nor too hard. It's just right for your current ability. As your skill level increases, the challenge needs to increase to keep you in flow and fully focused. This is illustrated in the following comments:

"My game is bridge, but I don't like playing with my neighbors. They have an irritating habit of always winning."

"I remember kayaking down the Colorado River and hitting those first big rapids. I was excited but in total control. It was great."

"I've had gardens so large I couldn't keep up with the weeds. It was frustrating. My garden now is just the right size. I can spend a morning out there and lose myself in planting and weeding and get everything done that needs doing."

5) A sense of self and the activity merge.

In flow, self-consciousness and self-awareness disappear. You get so caught up in the moment-to-moment flow that your sense of self and the activity merge.

"When I really get into a novel, when it's really good, it's like I'm part of it. I'm in the character's head, running down the same streets and alleys."

"When I was in college and a bunch of us got into one of those great intellectual conversations where facts and opinions were flying back and forth, we all had to pay attention. It was like the conversation had a life of its own and we were all a part of it."

"When I'm out jogging, I'm really not aware of anything else. It's like I'm floating along in my own rhythm."

6) You are unaware of distractions.

In flow, you are so absorbed that everything else disappears or fades into the background. Here are some descriptions of that state:

"When I'm standing above that golf tee, ready to hit that ball, I'm so focused on my stance and stroke that that's all I see."

"When I watch a movie I love, the couple next to me could be making love. It would take that much to pull me away from the movie and realize it was just a movie."

"I swim laps in the morning. Someone's always in the next lane, but I'm in my own little world. It's like the pool is all mine."

7) Anxiety dissipates.

In flow, you're not worried about success or failure. You're not worried about anything. You are simply doing. People describe this aspect of flow as follows:

"When I'm ice skating and know a difficult turn is coming up, I'm too busy anticipating that turn to worry about anything else."

"I give a fair number of lectures and speeches. When it's going well, when I'm really into it, there could be an audience of one or a thousand. There's no anxiety. It doesn't matter. I'm concentrating 100 percent on what I'm saying."

"When I'm playing my oboe and I notice a mistake right away, I usually get uptight. But when all is going smoothly, I don't worry about a thing. I just hear the music coming from that instrument."

8) Time is distorted.

In flow, the subjective experience of time is altered. You lose track of time. Minutes or hours fly by without realizing the clock is ticking. People describe this distorted sense of time this way:

"When I leave my newsgroup and my computer, I feel slightly dazed and disassociated. While I'm with the group, I lose all sense of time. What subjectively seems like twenty minutes turns out to be two-and-a-half hours."

"I love that feeling of being totally absorbed in what I'm doing, like looking at the clock and saying 'Dang, how can it be 4:00 a.m.—I just started this project!'"

"I felt so involved, it was like the time was a half hour. But it wasn't. It was more like three hours."

Flow and Performance

Psychologist Orjan de Manzano states that "expert performance is commonly accompanied by a subjective state of optimal experience called flow. Previous research has shown positive correlations between flow and quality of performance and suggests that flow may function as a reward signal that promotes practice."

That makes sense. Those who learn a musical instrument and enjoy practicing early on are more likely to feel the flow of playing than beginners who hate to practice. The same is true for sculpting or oil painting. Those who enjoy these activities from the moment they wrap their hands around a ball of clay or dab paint on a canvas are far more likely to feel the flow of painting and sculpting and continue learning and practicing. Flow is self-reinforcing.

In de Manzano's study of passion, he measured the heart rates, blood pressure, respiration, and muscle tension of classical pianists as they played and then asked them to rate their experience of flow. De Manzano's research results indicated that "seemingly effortless attention arises through an interaction between a positive effect and high concentration." Such seeming effortlessness is one of the hallmarks of flow.

After considering her list of potential passions, a Passion Discovery class member named Gloria decided that she was "finally going to get more involved with music." While participating in an exercise designed to bring up enjoyable memories, she recalled that she rarely missed watching the Master's Music Program on her local public television station. She described herself as always "straightening my backbone, smiling, and humming along." For Gloria, watching those programs and then buying the DVDs and watching them again and again, all the while paying attention to every detail, fit the definition of passion.

"The thing is though," she said, "I can hum a little, but I can't sing. I scare myself in the shower. So singing's out of the question." So she thought about purchasing and learning to play the piano instead of singing, but she didn't want to make that kind of investment until she was sure she would follow through. "I get bored easily," she admitted. "That's always been a problem for me—starting something, then dropping it before too long." So she logged onto craigslist and bought a used Yamaha keyboard and bench.

When she e-mailed Bruce several weeks after class asking for advice, she wrote that she had started her learning with free YouTube lessons. He advised her to complete a single lesson at a time and to learn it thoroughly before moving on to the next. He reminded her of flow requirements: specific doable steps and clear feedback, as well as matching skill with challenge. Each step could be a single YouTube lesson; the feedback would be whether she finished the lesson or not. Her immediate feedback would be successfully completing each step of the lesson, and even more immediate, how each note or chord sounded as she played it. He told her that learning should be both fun and challenging and that her anxiety should be moderate but not overwhelming.

Bruce reminded Gloria that playing a Bach concerto—a long-term goal she selected—might seem like an insurmountable challenge at first but not impossible since she would never actually have to play a Bach concerto. All she had to do was learn one more note, then one more chord and one more song. If she persisted, a Bach concerto would eventually emerge. If she got into the flow of playing, a Bach concerto would eventually play itself. As the nineteenth-century existentialist philosopher Friedrich Nietzsche once wrote, "He who would learn to run must first learn to stand and walk." The same is true with playing the piano, sailing a boat, flying an airplane, or any complicated task.

Most passionate activities move in and out of flow. When you're in the flow of singing, playing an instrument, or giving a speech, for example, you may be in flow until something in the audience draws your attention and breaks that flow. Should this occur, refocus and get into flow again.

Balanced Skill

The fourth element of flow that we described above is this: There is an even balance between challenge and skill. A sobering example is Anne of Cleves—the fourth of Henry VIII's six wives—who avoided the executioner's ax but found her marriage to King Henry annulled partially because she couldn't play a decent game of chess. After Henry's third wife, Jane Seymour, died in childbirth, princesses of childbearing age from Spain and France were considered, but political expedience ruled out those options, making Anne—a woman raised in the less sophisticated German court of Düsseldorf—Henry's wife number four.

Unfortunately for Anne—not to mention Henry—Henry found her physically unattractive. Also, Anne could not play a proper game of chess or cards, two of Henry's well-practiced passions. Luckily, by the age of forty-eight, Henry was obese, in constant pain from a festering leg wound, and likely suffering from erectile dysfunction. His failure to consummate the marriage with Anne was acceptable grounds for declaring the union null and void.

The problem was not simply that Anne played court

games poorly, as any novice would. The problem was, even as she learned, Henry's more advanced skills always outmatched hers. The fun of flow from an evenly matched challenge was never achieved during their short union.

A key component of the online fantasy game Guild Wars is balanced skills so that players are evenly challenged. The fun lies in combating someone of nearly equal ability. When that balance is achieved, players play for hours, locked into the flow of the game. According to psychology researchers Falko Rheinberg and Stefan Engeser, "One feels both optimally challenged and confident that everything is under control." In one of their experiments, Rheinberg and Engeser found that flow also depends on how important someone considers an activity. The more important someone feels the activity is, the more he tries his best to meet the increasing challenge. When he doesn't care, it doesn't matter. He doesn't try as hard.

Taming Distractions

Let's also talk a bit more about number 6 on the list of elements of flow: You are unaware of distractions. When you're fully engaged in the flow emanating from the exercise of a passion, distractions take a back seat. You either ignore or don't notice them. You're so laser-focused on what you're doing that you aren't aware of what's going on around you. As author and journalist Sue Halpern writes in Four Wings and a Prayer (2002), "Passion keeps one fully in the present, so that time becomes a series of mutually exclusive 'nows.'"

Serena Williams, the tennis superstar who has won more tennis trophies than any other woman in the history of the game, once said when asked about the flow of focused concentration, "If you can keep playing tennis when somebody is shooting a gun down the street, that's concentration." It's easy to observe Williams's single-minded concentration when she's playing in the Wimbledon finals. When she crouches, establishes her stance, and glares across the court, nothing else exists in her awareness—not the crowd, not the TV cameras, not even the line judge she may later admonish. Her full attention narrows to the subtle moves of her opponent and the ball held in her opponent's hand.

When that ball is tossed in the air, Williams senses where it is likely to fly and subtly leans in that direction. When her opponent strikes the ball, Williams follows its trajectory and spin as it hurtles toward her. Her own strike—at least it seems to her—is automatic from the muscle memory of years of practice. Williams' immediate goal is clear: hit the ball back. Her feedback is immediate: she either hits it or misses it and it does or doesn't go where she intended it to go. When her opponent's ability matches hers and they are both in top form—which is most often the case in the finals—either could win. Both players require the intense focus of flow to keep their play even.

In her own study of flow, sports psychologist Susan Jackson interviewed sixteen champion figure skaters who won national titles. Jackson found that it was focused concentration that temporarily set distractions aside for these athletes—starting flow and keeping it going.

Frank Sinatra once said he was always aware of the audience while waiting backstage and that he often wondered while waiting "if the voice was still there." But after he stepped out from behind the curtain and sang that first note, he said he got lost in the lyrics and the melody. "Throughout my career," he said in an interview, "if I have done anything, I have paid attention to every note and every word of every song I sang."

So what does this mean for us non-Sinatras and non-champions when we are truly in the flow of our passions? We know from research that distractions take a backseat once we get in flow; we also know that they can sometimes inhibit us from melding into that state. One thing we can do—as any serious college student knows who finds a quiet corner in the back of the library—is eliminate as many distractions as we can before we begin. Serena Williams's intense laser focus on the ball across the court caused everything else to disappear. Frank Sinatra waited in his dressing room until the last minute and then came out to start his song as the band struck up his introduction—leaving no time for distraction.

Assessing Your Flow

Are you aware of how well you flow in your passions? Evaluating yourself to become aware of this is worthwhile. To do this, re-examine the list of potential passions that you uncovered in Chapter 3. Select an activity that you are already passionate about or about which you think you could be passionate. See yourself being fully engaged in the activity and determine if it meets or could meet the requirements for flow we have just discussed:

The activity is done for its own sake—for the pure joy, fun, pleasure, and challenge of it.

The immediate goal is clear every step of the way.

You get precise and immediate feedback about how you're doing at each step.

There is a balance between your skill level and the challenge the activity requires.

At least on occasion, you lose awareness of self.

You're unaware of distractions or the passage of time.

Anxiety dissipates.

Time is distorted.

After an activity, you can usually judge the quality and intensity of flow. If you want to see how that might work, think about a time when you were in flow and rate that activity on the following scale.

Instructions: After involvement in a passion flow activity, you are able to say the following:

Don't Agree		Mostly Agree		Strongly Agree		
1	2	3	4	5	6	7

1. I was thoroughly focused.

1 2 3 4 5 6 7

3. I did not notice distractions.

1 2 3 4 5 6 7

4. I was easily able to concentrate.

1 2 3 4 5 6 7

5. Time passed without my awareness.

1 2 3 4 5 6 7

6. I felt focused and absorbed in what I was doing.

1 2 3 4 5 6 7

7. The challenge was just right for my skill level.

1 2 3 4 5 6 7

8. It all went very smoothly.

1 2 3 4 5 6 7

9. I felt in control.

1 2 3 4 5 6 7

10. I felt immersed in the activity.

1 2 3 4 5 6 7

Total Flow Score [ ]

Low Flow > 10 – 20
Medium Flow > 21 – 40
High Flow > 41 – 70

In psychologist Brennan Payne's investigation of flow in older adults, he found that the flow experienced in a passion can be experienced over and over during the course of a lifetime. Yet in order for that to happen, you have to more deliberately make it happen, both by choosing carefully what you do and by broadening your perspective on how you respond to existing conditions. When you choose to create time to engage in your passions, several of them during your lifetime, you are likely to spend more time in that heightened state of absorption and focus called flow.

Hopefully, in this chapter you've seen that although flow can be an essential ingredient in the experience of living and sustaining a passion, flow does not always happen automatically. There can be a real benefit for you in becoming more aware of how your true passions meet the common elements of flow so you can actively increase them. Doing things that are inherently rewarding for you, with some clear goals in mind; having a steady source of feedback; balancing your skill level with the level of challenge; and removing distractions are effective ways to stay in flow.

As Mike (Mihaly Csikszentmihalyi) writes, "In many ways, the secret to a happy life is to learn to get flow from as many passions as possible."

CHAPTER 14

Being In Gratitude

What does an attitude of gratitude have to do with passion? What is the connection between passion and gratitude? As the early twentieth-century British evangelist John Jowett wrote, "Life without thankfulness is devoid of passion." It's certainly true that the more passions you have -- since passions are about things you love -- the more you have to be grateful for.

Artist and glass sculptor Dale Chihuly says he's been passionate about the color and properties of glass ever since childhood and feels grateful every day that he is able to work in a medium he loves. He once said in an online interview, "I always say, take a little kid down to the beach-- you're walking along the beach, you're picking up shells, rocks, beautiful things, and then there's a little bit of sea glass, a little bit of a broken bottle -- blue, cobalt blue, green, some colors sitting there. The little kid is going to go for the glass every time." Chihuly is still that kid. He still walks along beaches, excited and grateful when a bit of color gleams up at him, and grateful that pursuing his early passion has allowed him to make a good living creating glass sculptures.

Basketball star and all-time scoring champion Kareem Abdul-Jabbar, after retiring from the game, took up a new passion -- presenting motivational talks and writing books to inspire others. He says he is grateful for the opportunity and then adds, "I think seeing one of my books in print has given me as much joy and sense of achievement as winning an NBA championship. Although I don't get the notoriety from my books that I've gotten as an athlete, it still gives me great joy to know that I can contribute something. To me, that's very meaningful and it gives me a lot of joy."

Attention To Gratitude

Few of us have Dale Chihuly's or Kareem Abdul-Jabbar's talent, fame or fortune for which to be grateful. The good news is that the research indicates we don't need it -- that what counts is the fact that we are grateful, not necessarily what we're grateful for. The more you lead a life of passion, no matter what its source, the more opportunity you have for gratefulness.

Psychologist Robert Emmons introduced his study of gratitude with the statement, "the ability to notice, appreciate, and savor the elements of one's life has been viewed as a crucial determinant of well-being." In one study of sixty-five adults suffering from congenital or adult-onset neuromuscular disease, Emmons found that those adults instructed to notice and then list daily events for which he or she felt grateful felt better than those who were assigned other tasks.

Examples from the "grateful things" group were:

"Just waking up in the morning and seeing the sun shine through my window."

"A friend who had a kind word for me."

"I exercised today and it felt good."

"I am grateful for my wonderful children and grandchildren."

"I am grateful for the Lord in my life."

"I still loved the old Rolling Stones song I heard on the radio."

None of these were big events. They were all little, here-and-there experiences that those in the "notice and appreciate" group, as a result of following their instructions, said they did notice and felt grateful for. These positive results are especially significant because this group suffered from the daily pain and distraction of chronic neuromuscular disease. Emmons and his research team concluded that "the gratitude experimental group exhibited a significantly heightened sense of well-being relative to the comparison groups. The effect on positive emotion appeared to be robust. The results suggest that a conscious focus on blessings may have emotional and interpersonal benefits."

If those benefits accrued to those in daily physical pain and discomfort, what are the implications for the rest of us?

Three Good Things

Referred to earlier, in one of Martin Seligman's first positive psychology studies, one experimental group was instructed to "each evening write down three good things that happened to you that day and why you think they happened." They were also asked in several ways to assess their mood throughout the day. Judgments of their mood and happiness were measured prior to the experimental procedure, one week after the start, and then again at one month, three month, and six month intervals. A control group was simply asked each evening to write a paragraph about "something that happened that day" -- whatever came to mind.

The results are shown in the graph below. The control/placebo "write something that happened that day" group had a spike in mood elevation immediately after given their initial instructions, perhaps anticipating that participation alone would raise their overall satisfaction. After that, their happiness ratings leveled off and ended up pretty much where they started.

The experimental, "three good things" group, (in black below), consistently improved in their overall happiness ratings throughout the six months of the experiment, rising steadily week-after-week and month-after-month.

The implication is clear. Be grateful for what you have as you go along, especially for the little things that happen most frequently -- the everyday things. The exercises in this chapter will help you get into the habit of doing just that.

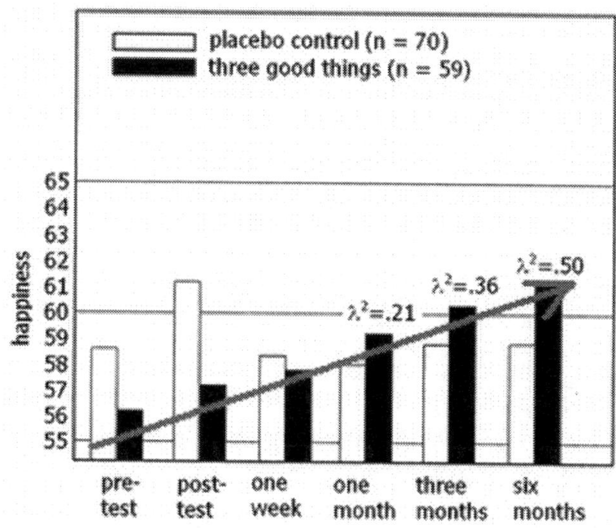

But wait a minute. Doesn't that advice contradict what we learned in the savoring chapter -- that reminiscing on past good times spurs good feelings? Not really. The difference is the "continue to reflect day after day," as Randy and Karin have explored by using the Five Minute Journal we mentioned in the last chapter. Reminiscing is good once in a while. It's the continual thinking of what was better in the past and comparing that to what you don't like in the present that gets you down, especially when your current "day-to-day" experiences are judged as less than or better than the past, a common mental habit for many people. And one we'd suggest you replace if you have it.

A Gratitude High

Psychologists Michael McCullough, Richard Emmons, and Jo-Ann Tsang set out to develop a scale that would help them measure overall feelings of gratitude that they could then use to measure the effect gratitude had on a sense of well-being. They began with a list of thirty-nine items that potentially measured gratitude and then paired that down to a six-item gratitude questionnaire designed to assess individual differences and experiences of gratitude. We won't use their research scale here, but the following self-evaluation serves the same purpose.

Later on, we'll be looking at specific kinds of gratitude along with methods for increasing gratitude, especially in areas in which you are passionate. But for now, take a look at where you stand overall. This is only for you, so be as honest as you can. You may want to come back and rate yourself again later to see how far you've come after completing the exercises that follow.

The Gratitude Scale

Don't Agree		Mostly Agree		Strongly Agree		
1	2	3	4	5	6	7

1. At least one thing has happened to me in the last day or the last week for which I feel thankful.

1 2 3 4 5 6 7

2. Even in a tough world, I still have much for which to be grateful.

1 2 3 4 5 6 7

3. I tend to look for things for which to be thankful

1 2 3 4 5 6 7

4. I never let days or weeks go by without being grateful for something or someone

1 2 3 4 5 6 7

5. I have lots of reasons to feel thankful…

1 2 3 4 5 6 7

6. Looking back at all that's happened to me in life, I have a lot to appreciate.

1 2 3 4 5 6 7

Total Gratitude Score ☐

Low Gratitude > 6 – 14
Medium Gratitude > 15 – 27

High Gratitude > 28 - 42

Negative Bias vs. An Attitude of Gratitude

Try this simple experiment. Find a piece of paper or open a blank computer page and quickly list as many words that occur to you in thirty seconds that have something to do with "emotion" or "kinds of emotion." Work quickly. Write as many as you can as fast as you can.

Now, go back over your list and put a checkmark next to all the words that have a positive connotation, such as "happy," "smile" or "glad," and an 'X' next to those that lean toward the negative side, like "sad," "depressed" or "angry." Add up your checkmarks and 'X's. You may have listed more positives than negatives, but most people end up with just the opposite -- with more negatives than positives, partly because human nature is biased toward the negative.

Those ancient cave men and women who skipped down the jungle trail whistling a happy tune, watching the clouds drift overheard, and thinking, "what's for lunch," were more often eaten for lunch than those who crept quietly, listening for telltale signs of danger. Those with an eye and an ear bent toward trouble had a better chance of surviving long enough to reproduce other alert trouble avoiders.

The brain in humans evolved as a problem solving mechanism, and the most pressing problem early humans faced was how to survive. "Nip trouble in the bud before it nips you" was nature's imperative, and thus today's bias toward the negative items on your list.

The Biased Human Brain

In one study by Jeff Larsen and T. A., the two

psychologists measured the brainwaves of subjects who viewed a series of positive pictures, negative pictures, and neutral pictures. The researchers found "larger amplitude brain potentials" when viewing negative stimuli than either neutral or positive. In summarizing their findings, they found "overwhelming support for the hypothesis that negativity bias in affective processing (1) weights more heavily than positive and (2) occurs early in the initial categorization."

In their Evolutionary Psychology: A Primer, Leda Cosmides and John Tooby summarize three principle reasons for an evolutionary bias toward negativity.

Principle One: "The brain is a physical system. It functions as a computer. Its circuits are designed to generate behavior that is appropriate to the environmental circumstance."

Principle Two: "Neural circuits were designed by natural selection to solve problems that our ancestors faced during our species' evolutionary history."

Principle Three: "Survival of the individual and of the species is the prime directive."

Psychologist Chris Hsee puts it starkly and succinctly. "We are not really built to be happy. We are built to survive."

Roy Baumeister and Ellen Bratslavsky summed up the evidence for a negative human bias when they wrote, "The greater power of bad events over good ones is found in everyday events, major life events, close relationship outcomes, social network patterns, interpersonal interactions, and learning processes. Bad emotions, bad parents, and bad feedback have more impact than good ones, and bad information is processed more thoroughly than good. The self is more motivated to avoid bad self-definitions than to pursue good ones. Bad impressions and bad stereotypes are quicker to form and more resistant to disconfirmation than good ones. Hardly any exceptions (indicating greater power of good) can be found. Taken together, these findings suggest that bad is stronger than good, as a general principle across a broad range of psychological phenomena."

Randy remembers his early days teaching university psychology and sociology courses when at the end of the semester, he'd go over student evaluations and take delight in positive comments made about his teaching style and what students got out of the course when all of a sudden he'd spot a critical comment and the wind would be taken right out of his sails-- at least for the moment and even sometime later he'd find himself obsessing on one or two negative comments.

Baumeister and Bratslavsky go on to say that "this may in fact be a general principle or law of psychological phenomena, possibly reflecting the innate predispositions of the psyche or at least reflecting the almost inevitable adaptation of each individual to the exigencies of daily life."

They conclude by writing, "In our review, we have found bad to be stronger than good in a disappointingly relentless pattern. More over, good can still triumph in the end by force of numbers. Even though a bad event may have a stronger impact than a comparable good event, many lives can be made happy by virtue of having far more good than bad events."

What's the bottom line? What does all this mean for you? It's hard to feel passionate when you're unconsciously scanning for negativity, but awareness is power. When you catch yourself scanning for what's wrong or what could go wrong, set a limit. Run down your mental checklist, then set it aside and get fully involved in what's positive.

Accumulating Gratitude

In an ordinary, everyday situation or relationship in which most things go well, your attention, by human nature, will still be naturally drawn to what doesn't go well. After all, why pay attention to what's right since it doesn't need fixing? Why not focus on what isn't fixed or what still needs to be done. As a result, at the end of an ordinary day, you will have emotionally noticed and banked away the problems, frustrations, incompletes and still-to-be-dones of the day and overlooked or taken for granted what was good, what was right, and what worked. You tend to save up and cart around the heavy weight of negative memory and negative experience rather than floating on the positive lightness that buoys you up. As George Barnard Shaw once said, "Life is one damn thing after the other." Shaw was right, but only partly. Life can also be one good thing after the other if you work around human nature and make it a habit to notice the positives. Randy says that's also a part of our human evolutionary imperative. It's called "free will," when humans exercise the choice to focus on the positive, a habit that requires regular practice like any other learned behavior.

Banking Good Things

Good things occur in three ways. First, you naturally stumble across them in the course of an ordinary day. You get up and happen to look out the window at an especially beautiful sunrise, or someone thanks you for a favor you hadn't known you'd done them, or you see an especially fascinating program on Public TV that draws you in and inspires you.

Good things also happen deliberately when you take some action to make them happen. Leslie, a dental assistant in a Passion Discovery workshop, after listing "travel" as a new passion she planned to pursue, told the class that she intended to book "two passionate nights for me and my husband" in a luxury suite at the Princeville Hotel in Kauai, Hawaii, a resort, she said, that Conde Nast ranked as one of the ten best in the world. From the twinkle in her eye, I got the idea that she meant "passion" in all senses of the word and that she intended to use the techniques she had learned in the workshop -- focused attention, savoring, and all the rest -- to extract as much delight, pleasure, and appreciation as she could from both her travels and her marriage.

If Leslie followed through with her plans -- and she convinced the class that she would – she likely ended up standing on the deck of the Princeville Hotel at sunset, sipping a drink and looking across Hanalei Bay. The class was sure that moment, deliberately created, would be one she would remember with fondness for years to come.

Of course, it's possible and even likely that a few bad things will happen on the way to Kauai and the Princeville Hotel. The airline might lose their luggage, or a baby seated directly behind them might whine and cry all the way across the Pacific. And even after their arrival, she might notice that paradise sometimes has cracks in the sidewalk and that untended weeds grow up between the palm trees. Her mood, especially with her inherent, human negative bias, won't simply depend on what happened. It will partly depend on what she noticed or focused on with all the myriad stimuli around her.

Leslie could spend her time in Hawaii worrying about how her fourteen year old daughter was doing with her grandparents back home, or whether or not she had turned the thermostat down in the house, or stopped the delivery of their newspaper and mail, or if she was spending too much money for the luxury hotel suite. Before taking a Passion Discovery class, she might have worried about many things that could go wrong while they were away. But instead, based on what she'd learned, she was determined to review her checklist one final time and then deal with whatever "could" happen only if and when it "did" happened. In the meantime, until she learned otherwise, she would focus on savoring and being grateful for all the good things Hawaii had to offer.

Leslie's potential worry-list reminded us of another George Bernard Shaw quote. When Shaw was an old man -- he lived to ninety-three – several ladies clubs in Dublin kept inviting him to speak at dinners, realizing that each talk could be his last. At one event near the end of his life, but not nearly his last gasp, he is quoted as saying, "I've lived a long life and worried about many things." After a telling pause, he added, "Most of which never happened."

Emotionally, worrying about what might happen is the same as if it did happen. The body can't tell the difference. Physiologically, worry churns tension and raises blood pressure. Real or imagined, the effects accumulate and extract a toll on the body. Psychologically, worry dampens subjective well-being, or S.W.B., as psychologists call it. You pay the price of anxiety and distraction for worry even when your teenager is perfectly safe and having fun at home, even when your thermostat actually is turned down, even when the newspapers and mail are safely waiting for you at the carrier's, and even when your vacation budget is well within acceptable limits.

Spending time worrying about what doesn't need to be fixed or can't be fixed grinds down an attitude of gratitude and blocks your ability to notice and appreciate the beauty or goodness that surround you. Worry and anxiety take their toll on passion because it's hard to lose yourself in passion when you're focused on your worries.

Randy finds great value in the work of psychologist Rick Hansen. In Hansen's book, Buddha's Brain, he compares the para-sympathetic nervous system's "fight or flight" response with the brain's sympathetic nervous system, with its tendency to slow down rather than speed up physiological processes. Hansen points out that our caveman "fight or flight," anxiety response is no longer a reaction to the external, environmental threat, but more often a parasympathetic response to our internal environment, to our thoughts of fear or danger, to natural bias in a negative direction.

After Effects

Bruce reports on the results he experienced with his own gratitude experiment:

"I notice the effects of negative bias in myself. One of the reasons I'm passionate about teaching the psychology of passion is that I get to apply what I teach to myself. When I first read about the uplifting effects of keeping an account of things for which you felt gratitude, I went out and bought a leather-bound journal. I sat it next to my bed as a reminder, and then, just before turning out the light and drifting off at night, I thought back on the day and tried to recall five events or moments that I felt grateful for that day. The first two or three usually came easy. After that, I initially had to think a little harder to come up with five.

Soon after I started keeping the journal, I noticed my mind skipping over most of the irritations of the day. That wasn't my self-assigned task. I was scanning the day's experience for shiny nuggets that stood out among the ordinary pebbles and sharp rocks in the day's landscape. When an irritation came to mind, I brushed it aside. I also noticed that I wasn't thinking about any uncompleted tasks or what I had to do the next day. My mind was too busy focusing on what went right that day. After laying my journal aside and turning out the light, I fell asleep with pleasant thoughts and images. I woke up in a better mood, often with a grin on my face as the new day dawned, knowing I would be looking for good things that day too.

Throughout the first week, I found myself noticing more little things for which to be grateful -- the slanted angle evening shadow as it fell across a building, a friendly face as I passed someone on the sidewalk, the feel of a soft rug beneath my feet -- all the while knowing I would have to come up with something to write in my journal that night. I had come to a better understanding of Albert Schweitzer's dictum, "To educate yourself for the feeling of gratitude means to take nothing for granted."

My own gratitude journal experience dovetails with the accumulating psychological research that says deliberately engaging in an attitude of gratitude increases overall life satisfaction by drawing your attention to things for which to be grateful. And, gratitude is related to passion -- first, by stimulating an appetite for passion, and second, by directing your attention to areas in which passion might be found, then keeping your attention on those passions which in turn creates more gratifying experiences. It becomes a positive feedback loop."

The Proof of Gratitude

The sum of numerous research studies shows that nurturing and fostering an attitude of gratitude increases the frequency and duration of positive feelings while decreasing negative ones. Practicing gratitude as a daily habit reinforces a positive outlook on life that adds up to an increased sense of overall satisfaction. Keeping a gratitude journal reinforces a gratitude habit.

Journaling

We've already briefly talked about the value of journaling in the chapter on Savoring. Here are some ideas for going deeper and getting the most out of journaling specifically on gratitude.

Keeping a gratitude journal requires spending a few minutes each day focusing on the good things that happened that day. As soon as you start, you are immediately aware of more grateful feelings. Even on a bad day, you find a few good things. After several days, those who kept a journal commonly reported a brighter mood that stretched throughout the day. They lingered more in pleasant moments. They appreciated the day's events again as they recalled them in the evening to write in their journal.

If you'd like to try keeping a gratitude journal, here are the steps…

1) ***Buy a blank notebook and pace it next to your bed with a pen readily available.***

Throughout the day, be more aware of things or events,

big or small but mostly small, for which you are grateful. Make a mental note or a real note. These are often instances that make you feel good and lift your spirits, things that you usually take for granted -- the surprisingly light traffic on the way to the office, a great tasting sandwich for lunch, the fresh smell of the morning dew on the grass, the call from an old friend to make plans for a get together. It's those moments you may have stopped to savor.

Notice how simply adopting a grateful attitude draws your attention toward the positive and shifts it away from the negative. Notice how you tend to be a little less critical and more accepting.

Each night at bedtime, think back a minute and list five things for which you are grateful that day. List them briefly, expanding your description later if you feel like it. Savor each experience before noting the next, or jot them all down quickly and then go back and savor them one at a time.

Turn the nightlight out and drift off to sleep with an image or thought of each grateful moment. (As you fall asleep, your may think of other gratitude moments but don't wake yourself up to jot them down. Just drift off with those in mind.)

2) ***At the end of the week, or at some regular time of your choosing, look back at what you've written and ask yourself...***

How do I feel as I think back on these positive events now?

What themes do I notice? What kinds of events naturally arouse my gratitude?

Are my feelings of gratitude something I want to share with a loved one or someone I care for? If that loved one is keeping their own gratitude journal, is there some event or pattern that they might they want to share with me? Do I dare share? Do I dare ask?

3) Be persistent in keeping your journal at the beginning.

Commit to writing every night for at least two weeks. Five things to be grateful for each day may be hard to come up with at first, but after a few days you will be surprised at how much you begin to notice and how many opportunities spontaneously arise. You may find that you are grateful for the same things several days in a row -- a great workout, a tasty breakfast, a good night's sleep or sleeping next to your partner or spouse, for example. That's fine. Just list them again as a continuing source of gratitude.

After a while, you may find that noticing small positive events becomes a habit and that you only need to write in your journal two or three nights a week instead of every night, and then perhaps only once a week as you strengthen your habit of noticing and appreciating good things. If you stop keeping your journal and find your attitude of gratitude slipping, start again as a regular night-time ritual until gratitude is reignited.

A Few Good Things

Here are few examples of moments of gratitude shared in a Passion Discovery Class…

"Watching my children at the dinner table and realizing how quickly they grow up and how much I will miss them when those chairs are empty."

"It was an unusually warm day for October. I rode my bike and smelled the fresh air."

"I came across one of those big picture books of Ireland in the bookstore. I thumbed through it slowly, then came back and looked through it again. It was a wonderful two minute vacation."

"My cat sitting in my lap in the evening."

"Watching the distressing economic news on TV and realizing how lucky I am to have a job."

"My husband told me how my soft my hair was and how good it smelled. He noticed! He loves me!"

It's not usually the big things that make each day a better day. It's the little ordinary things that happen here and there.

Gratitude and Passion

Look back at the lists of possible passions you developed in Chapter 4. The point of that Passion Discovery exercise was to uncover potential passions that you might have forgotten or of which you weren't fully aware. As you review that list now, you may find that many of the things you are grateful for and the passions on your list overlap -- that you tend to be grateful for things you also feel passionate about. If you're passionate about playing tennis or golf, for example, it's easy to feel grateful for an opportunity to play a game. If you're a wine connoisseur, you're likely to appreciate discovering a great vintage and savoring that first glass. If you are passionate about spending time with your children or grandchildren, special time together, a good visit or even an unexpected call or letter from those no longer near leaves a lot to be grateful for. Practicing gratitude invites you to notice and savor more small events within and outside of your passions and to discover more about which passions are strongest within you.

Living Fully in the Present

In one study of gratitude, psychologist Phillip Watkins found that considering one's mortality tends to sharpen feelings of gratitude for small, seemingly inconsequential events by viewing them in a larger perspective. Experimental subjects who were occasionally reminded of their eventual demise were more grateful for simply being alive or for everyday events like eating a great meal. By occasionally reminding themselves that life is short, they began purposely extracting more from what was available each day. They also began taking better care of themselves -- eating better and getting more exercising.

When Dr. Watkins presents his findings to an audience, he often asks them, "Does thinking about your own death make you appreciate your life a little more?" and then gives them a moment to ponder his question. He then tells them, "Gratitude is the amplifier of the good. Like a guitar amp that makes the music sound louder, or a magnifying glass that magnifies an object to make it appear larger, gratitude brings out the goodness in people to make it larger, greater and stronger."

As you reach the end of this chapter, consider for a moment all the things you have to be grateful for, and then ask yourself what would happen if you thoughtfully appreciated them a little more often. And what if you only had another day to do so?

Chapter 15

Meaning and Passion

Is being passionate or passionately engaged with something by itself enough for a good life, or does a good life also require a deeper sense of meaning? In one study of life satisfaction, psychologists Christopher Peterson and Nansook Park concluded that the pursuit of meaning was "much more predictive of life satisfaction than the pursuit of pleasure."

Martin Seligman, after writing his book Authentic Happiness (2004), concluded that passions are wonderful but not all we need to make us happy. An avid bridge player, Marti noticed that some tournament players didn't seem particularly joyous or happy while playing. They rarely smiled even when they won and often huddled by themselves between games. Some even cheated to win. So if they didn't seem to play for the pleasure of the game, Marti wondered, why did they play? As a psychologist thinking like a psychologist and observing them for a while, he concluded that at least some of them played for a sense of accomplishment—they played to win for the sake of winning. It was more winning than the process of playing that they were passionate about.

In Mike's follow-up book, Character Strengths and Virtues (Peterson and Seligman 2004), he identified accomplishment, or mastery of something, as one of the elements he felt was needed for a "fully flourishing life." A second element was passion. A third was meaning and purpose, an element on which University of Virginia psychologists Shigehiro Oishi and Selin Kesebir agree. Oishi and Kesebir define the search for meaning as "the strength, intensity, and activity of someone's desire and efforts to establish and/or augment their understanding of the significance and purpose of their lives."

These psychologists summarize a lengthy list of psychological research that has consistently found a positive relationship between "a perceived meaning in life" and a wide range of measures of life satisfaction. They conclude that their findings "appear to support the widely held opinion that meaning in life is universally important to experiencing well-being and living a satisfying life."

Nonetheless, their research has also led them to conclude that what constitutes meaning in life varies widely from person to person and that meaning's relative importance also varies. While some feel at a loss without meaning, others find the whole concept of meaning meaningless. As Vaclav Havel—the Czech playwright, essayist, poet, dissident, and politician—once said, "The tragedy of modern man is not that he knows less and less about the meaning of his own life, but that it bothers him less and less."

Let's explore the relationship between meaning and passion.

The Meaning of Meaning

At a recent visit for a dental checkup, when Bruce's dentist asked him if he had any questions, he said, "Yes—what's the meaning of life?" Bruce thought she would say, "Clean teeth with no cavities," but she didn't. She said, "To be happy." Bruce thought that was a pretty good answer. If he had been more serious about his question, he might have asked her, "What is the meaning of life for you?"

The ultimate meaning of life is a religious or

philosophical question beyond the scope of psychology. Happiness, satisfaction, and well-being, however, are within the realm of psychological investigation, as is an individual's concept of meaning, whatever its ultimate source.

There are two ways to conceive of meaning. The first is, how do we fit into the larger reality of everything? The second, more earthly, conception is, what is the meaning of someone's life as he or she lives it? The second conception of meaning is sometimes referred to by philosophers as the anthill meaning, which states that ants have no way of knowing who or what created them, but they know (at least biologically) that their inherent purpose in life is to carry a breadcrumb from one spot on a kitchen floor, across that kitchen, out under the screen door, across the backyard, and down into the anthill—and then deposit it there before turning around and heading back to the kitchen for another breadcrumb.

So breadcrumb carrying may be an ant's purpose—but is "purpose" the same as "meaning"? Some would say it is; they believe that the meaning of life is God-given and the purpose is to follow His commandments. Others say that there is no inherent meaning or purpose in life—that the purpose of life is to find your purpose, which could mean discovering what you are inherently good at and feel passionate about, and then pursuing it, whatever its origin. The subtitle of Janet Bray Attwood and Chris Attwood's best-selling The Passion Test book is The Effortless Path to Finding Your Life Purpose. Why and how do they make a claim about an effortless path? Using breadcrumbs as a metaphor, they say that when you discover your passions, they can become the breadcrumbs that lead you to your life purpose. Get clear about and live your passions and you will, by their definition, be on your own unique life path, the one most meaningful for you.

Do We Need Meaning?

Can fulfilling a passion really help us achieve purpose and meaning? Jesus' purpose and meaning was fulfilling the mission that God sent him to earth to fulfill. No one can deny the passion and purpose of any of the great religious leaders—Jesus, Muhammad, Moses, Buddha, Lao Tzu (the founder of Taoism), and others. At some point in their lives, they had little doubt about what to do when they awoke each morning. Their purpose and meaning were one and the same. The one flowed from the other.

For most of us—unless we happened to be born a Mahatma Gandhi or a Mother Teresa—the purpose and meaning of life is not quite so clear, and it's not usually something we think about on a daily basis. In the daily grind of life, our purpose is sometimes to simply maneuver over and around the challenges and roadblocks to get through the day. But is getting through the day enough for a satisfying life? Is constantly hauling breadcrumbs from point A to point B like ants nothing but meaningless drudgery? And is adding joy and passion to breadcrumb carrying enough for a satisfying life?

For some, it is. For others, surveys indicate that life has no meaning—at least none that they dwell on. It's often the case that dwelling too much on meaning—or the lack thereof—not only results in a fixated frustration but actually creates a black cloud of depression.

So how important is meaning to a satisfying life? It turns out to be important if you feel you need meaning and don't have any. If you think life, and your life in particular, has no meaning and meaning is important to you, it's hard to lead a satisfying life, let alone a happy one.

The Changing Meaning of Meaning

In the mid-to-late fifties, a ragtag group of bright young artists, painters, musicians, and writers ventured in from all over the country and congregated in Manhattan's Greenwich Village—The Village, as they called it. And that's exactly what it became: a congregation of inspired young villagers, all of whom supported one another and who were there for the same reason: to escape the mundane reality and pedestrian life in their hometowns and discover personal meaning through their art and their writing, "free from the constraints of normal society."

That list of youthful unknowns eventually became the Who's Who of the decade: James Baldwin, Joan Didion, John Gregory Dunne, Allen Ginsberg, Jack Kerouac, Norman Mailer, Gay and Nan Talese, Calvin Trillin, and Mark van Doren, among others. They all had a purpose. That purpose was to express themselves. "We thought it was a good thing to sit around and write poetry all day," writer Dan Wakefield, a member of that group, recalls in retrospect. "We were Bohemians, and we developed a lifestyle around that."

So where are the Villagers now? What happened to their purpose and meaning? History happened. Historical events shifted to bring forth a sense of national purpose and meaning. The Vietnam War heated up in the sixties. Civil rights activists started marching in Mississippi and Alabama and found themselves hosed down, attacked by dogs, and hauled off to jail. Sitting around in a Village basement, getting looped on cheap wine, and discussing the meaning of offbeat poetry suddenly seemed shallow. The emerging meaning was now to be found by putting yourself and your beliefs on the line, not in writing or in intellectual discussions—unless you wrote freedom songs or carried a banner in the frontline of a march.

Even the emerging folk singers, who cut their teeth and sharpened their voices in Village pubs, urged action beyond the cloistered village. "We shall overcome" came to mean we should help overcome. Robert Allen Zimmerman—newly christened in the Village as Bob Dylan—pleaded in his unique raspy voice, "How many years must a mountain exist before it's washed to the sea? How many years can some people exist before they're allowed to be free?" Dylan and his friend Joan Baez took their songs on the road in the March on Washington, a major Civil Rights event in 1963.

It was around that time, Wakefield laments, that "the meaning of Village life changed. The beat generation was over. We weren't rebelling anymore. We were copying ourselves. We were becoming the standard. So the ones of us that were writers went on to selling books."

A younger crop of flower children created their own offbeat scenario on the opposite coast, in Haight-Ashbury in San Francisco. The meaning of life for the Love Generation was found in talking about love and making love. They naively assumed that if everyone followed their example, the world would evolve into a warless and loving place. When the world's armies didn't turn their guns in for flower seeds, the love children's passion for universal love began to cool.

At the same time, spontaneous free love with anyone and everyone they ran across spread suspicion and jealously like the plague. Haight-Ashbury itself gradually morphed back into a low-rent district, and many of the former love children either re-registered for college or continued smoking pot and making a living selling handmade leather belts to tourists roaming San Francisco's Galleria.

To its credit, the Love Generation created an awareness

of the importance of peace, love, and understanding in a seemingly hostile world—one that was not lost and that today one can see in everything from community gardens to farmer's markets, smart and sustainable planning and development, and even open-source software. These are diverse expressions of that mid-twentieth century revolution. Meaning shifted and morphed again as this Baby Boomer generation grew up and began to change the world on a larger set and scale.

A New Mind Experiment

Students in Bruce's Positive Psychology college course are invited to participate in a mind experiment. They're asked to imagine that they were deceased and that beneath their name and the dates on their gravestone they had two choices—and only two. The stone engravers could either etch "I was successful" or "I was happy." The experiment was a setup, of course: we would all prefer both. But given a forced choice, most would choose happy over successful. Some would even argue that success without happiness is no success at all.

It's certainly true that passion is, or can be, an important component of a meaningful life. In fact, it's hard to imagine a meaningful life devoid of passion. But as we've seen, all passions are not equal. A passion for pizza may very well be a major component in the meaning of life for John Schnatter, the CEO of Papa John's, but it probably doesn't provide a lot of meaning for you, even if you love pizza.

Try this mind experiment at this point on your journey. It has no obvious answer. Ask yourself, if your life were to end suddenly before the sun rose tomorrow, what few words or what phrase might sum up the meaning of your life as it currently stands? What could be etched on the front of your gravestone that would succinctly summarize that current meaning, and what clarification or addition might be etched on the back? Consider your answer and write it down before asking yourself the following questions:

How easy or difficult was it to come up with a brief statement of the meaning of your life as it stands right now? Did a phrase or a few words quickly occur to you, or did you have to think about it?

Does the clarification statement etched on the back match, add to, subtract from, or subvert what's on the front?

Are you satisfied with what that summary statement says to those you love and care for, as well as to future descendants who might visit your grave and read it?

Would you change it if you could? If so, what would you like it to say at the end of your life?

What could you do between now and then that would lead to a more satisfying summary?

This discussion brings to mind the death of Ray Bradbury, the famous science fiction writer and author of Fahrenheit 451. It was reported by ABC News via Twitter that Mr. Bradbury requested the following statement be engraved on his tombstone: "Here lies a man who loved life from beginning to end and is sorry it's over." Now, there's a man who lived a life of passion, meaning, and accomplishment.

Another approach that can get you to a similar place of awareness about what may be missing in your life now is actually visualizing what could have happened by the time you reach the age of 100. In the book The Passion Test, the authors invite readers to write out their 100th birthday speech. In this imaginary scenario, you visualize and write about where you are, whom you're with, how you got there, and what happened along the way, leading up to your most wonderful birthday bash.

Satisfaction, Meaning, and Regrets

Bruce asked a friend of his what her passions were, and at first she said, "I'm not sure. I don't think I have any." He goes on to say this:

She conceded that was not entirely true when I reminded her that she loved to seek out treasures at garage sales, read mystery books, and see the latest movies on opening night. I added that she wouldn't know what to do with herself if those activities were suddenly forbidden.

"Oh, sure, those things," she said. "But that's not enough."

Not enough, I wondered. Not enough for what? What's missing? Before retirement, she had been employed as the chief administrative assistant for the president of a regional utility company. "Everything that came through that office came through me," she was proud to say. Knowing her, I also knew it was important that she was the chief administrative assistant to the president, not just any administrative assistant to any manager. It was as if in that exalted position, she felt valued and useful. After retirement, when asked what she did, she always said, "I'm retired," then quickly added, "I used to be the chief administrative assistant to the president of the company"—as if to say, "I used to be someone important." There's no doubt that much of her self-image and the day-to-day meaning of her life had come from her career.

But did she consider her job a passion? Did it fit the five-part definition of a passion? Was it something that she valued and loved, that she had a strong inclination toward, that she spent a good deal of time at, and that defined her?

Knowing her, I would say, yes. She loved her job and couldn't wait to go into the office each morning. It's clear her work defined her and still does. She had other passions, but after retirement they weren't enough to replace that huge loss of satisfaction and self-definition. She needed something else to provide personal meaning and was still in search of that something.

British philosopher Bertrand Russell wrote, "The more things a man is interested in, the more opportunities for happiness he has, and the less he is at the mercy of fate, since if he loses one thing he can fall back upon another." But it's not simply the number or frequency of passions that make for a good life—although the number of passions play a significant part of that. It's whether you feel they add up to something that means something to you. As Mihaly Csikszentmihalyi wrote in Good Business, "A good life consists of more than simply the totality of enjoyable experiences. It must also have a meaningful pattern, a trajectory of growth that results in the development of increasing emotional, cognitive, and social complexity."

Actress, social advocate, and exercise guru Jane Fonda, who has kept changing her self-definition her entire life, wrote in her latest book, Prime Time (2011), that when she was turning sixty she felt that she was entering her "last" act. "Well," she wrote, "if that's the case, and if what I'm scared of isn't death but getting to the end with regrets, then I've got to figure out what would be the things that I would regret if I hadn't done them or achieved them by the end of my last act. And they were: having an intimate relationship and having made a difference." She turned to determining how she could inject meaning into that last act.

Bronnie Ware, an experienced palliative care nurse in

Australia, asks her patients about any regrets they have as they face their last days of life. She recorded what people shared in what became a popular blog, Inspiration and Chai, later putting her observations in the book The Top Five Regrets of the Dying (2012). She says that people wished they'd had the courage to live a life true to themselves, not the life others expected of them; they wished they hadn't worked so hard (this is especially true for men); they wished they'd had the courage to express their feelings; they wished they'd stayed in better touch with friends; and they wished they'd let themselves be happier.

Ware asks, "What's your greatest regret so far, and what will you set out to achieve or change before you die?"

Waiting for Meaning

The results of a series of psychological investigations have shown that there is no single component of happiness and satisfaction, but rather a recipe of ingredients that includes a mix of goals, satisfying social relationships, passions, and a sense meaning. But if meaning—that final ingredient—is important to you, how do you find it? Where do you look?

In Samuel Beckett's classic play Waiting for Godot, Vladimir and Estragon, the two main characters, anxiously wait along the road for someone named Godot, whom neither has met but both have heard of and think they will recognize when they see him. Others pass along the road who think they may have seen Godot but aren't quite sure. One passerby isn't sure if Godot even exists. In the meantime, Vladimir and Estragon grow older and Godot never does appear. They spend their lives waiting for Godot.

Psychologist and researcher Michael Steger writes in

Psychology Today that people often act like Vladimir and Estragon, passively waiting for meaning to come along the road, poke them in the chest, and shout, "Here I am! Here's your meaning!" Steger writes, "My research shows two trends. First, people who are open-minded and active in their approach to life seem to search for meaning in their lives in a positive and healthy way. Second, people who already feel their lives are rich in meaning and who are seeking deeper meaning are more satisfied with their lives." Steger concludes that those who actively seek meaning or who already have a sense of meaning that they actively deepen are more satisfied with their lives than those who take no action in finding or deepening meaning. The key words are actively seek. Meaning, then, is dependent upon whether or not it is sought and/or deepened as an active part of one's life.

For some, actively seeking has been a matter of life and death. Randy remembers reading and being inspired by Viktor Frankl's book Man's Search for Meaning in his freshman year of college. Frankl was in a concentration camp in Nazi Germany during World War II, wondering when he would be exterminated. In that most hideous and powerless situation and environment, Frankl had an epiphany that no matter the external conditions, he always had a choice of what to think and what meaning he made of his experience. This was his ultimate freedom in a place where you wouldn't suspect any kind of freedom could exist.

Likewise, Nelson Mandela, a freedom advocate and leader in South Africa who was confined to an island prison for decades, was determined not to have his spirit broken. How did he do that? One way was to grow a garden and feed his prison guards while realizing he still had a larger purpose to fulfill.

Hopefully you won't ever have to be subjected to such extreme conditions for you to come to a deeper sense of meaning and purpose in your life.

A Personal Sense of Meaning

Perhaps the question shouldn't be "What is the meaning of life?" but rather, "What is the meaning of life for you at your particular stage of life?" It's a hugely personal question that's not always easy to answer and not often asked. And yet, no one wants to be near the end of life and say or think, "My life had no meaning."

When Connie Chung interviewed Marlon Brando several years before he died, she asked him about death. Brando replied, "I don't mind dying. That doesn't bother me. I even know what I'll say if I know the end's coming. I'll say, 'What the hell was that all about?'"

Would you want to be asking, "What the hell was that all about?" at the end of your life?

Bruce tells this story about his father's sense of meaning and purpose:

My father was not the type to ask or contemplate that type of question, even when his cancer treatment was discontinued and he knew he didn't have long to live. I had grown closer to him after my mother, his wife of fifty-six years, died three years earlier. I arranged my therapy schedule so I could spend more time with him. We talked openly about death and how lonely he had been without my mother. When he fell in his home and was no longer able to live safely on his own, he was confined to a wheelchair and reluctantly let himself be admitted to a nursing home.

I saw him the week before he died. He was sleeping

peacefully and unaware I was there, but when I visited the time before, he was alert and fully himself. "Dad," I said. "Let's get out of this place and get a cold beer."

"Will they let me?"

"It's not a jail. They can't stop us."

As a psychologist, I knew the procedures. I knew they couldn't stop us, but I got permission from the nursing home physician anyway. I had a male nurse help me get Dad in a wheelchair and into the car. We found a local pub and managed to maneuver into a wheelchair-accessible booth.

"What about my meds?" Dad asked.

"I checked. You can have a beer."

We talked about old times and the places we had lived while my brother and I were growing up. It was our farewell conversation and we both knew it. Dad knew the meaning of his life. Unlike Marlon Brando, he had no need to ask, "What the hell was it all about?" He knew what it was all about: it was about being a good husband and father.

He was buried next to my mom, just as they'd planned before she died. They'd only left the date of dad's death to be chiseled on their joint tombstone. Everything else was in place and waiting. If I had asked him—which I didn't, although I often ask a client—what few words or what phrase he would like engraved on his tombstone that would sum up what he was most proud of, what had meant the most to him, I know that he would have said, without hesitation, "Put down 'Husband and Father.'" And if I had asked what else he would write on the back of that stone, he would have said, "It wasn't always easy."

At the time of this writing, Randy's father, Tom, is nearing ninety and his mother is eighty-six. They are living where Randy used to live in Trinidad, a small town in

Northern California. Randy's mother, Ellen, has had Type II diabetes since middle age. Her body has literally fallen apart, while his dad still jogs, bikes, and kayaks. Still, at their age, his parents jointly manage a considerable-size rental business of several homes and buildings in two towns nearby.

When asked why they still choose to deal with so many headaches at this stage of life, they tell Randy that they like to solve problems together and that they "want to take care of their tenants." And they really do, despite some very difficult cases and situations. They understand that despite the inevitabilities of age and the obstacles of disease, having some sort of shared meaning and purpose not only gives them something to do, it provides a genuine sense of usefulness that keeps them going and gets them through their day.

Here are some of the meaning-of-life answers that have arisen in Passion Discovery classes:

> "I want to pick a major in college that serves a purpose."

> "The most important thing to me is raising my daughter to be a decent person."

> "Now that I'm retired and not working, I can finally figure out what I want to do."

> "The meaning of life to me is to be the best therapist and counselor that I can be."

> "My husband is dead. I'm not sure how to go on without him."

"More and more, as I grow older, I want to serve God."

If you're unsure of what the meaning of life might be for you, here are some questions you might contemplate to narrow down your quest:

If you were asked to teach someone the essence of life, what would you teach?

When you really think about it, what are your deepest values?

Which family members, leaders, mentors, or others do you admire, and why? What is it about them or what they've done? What have you learned from their example that could add or inspire meaning in your own life?

When people come to you for help, what help or advice are they seeking? What do they see in you that would lead them to seek that type of aid or advice? Do you see any meaning in having that wisdom, knowledge, understanding, or talent?

At the end of your life, what would you regret not having done? If you accomplished that between now and then, what meaning would it add?

What cause or causes do you strongly believe in?

Given your talents, passions, and values, how could you more often use them to contribute something of meaning or value to yourself or others?

More Than Passion

David Leap, the superintendent of an inpatient mental hospital where Bruce once worked, loved his job. He was the first superintendent born and raised on the Eastern Shore of Maryland. David had grown up with many of the patients' families. He had gone to high school with some of their brothers or sisters and attended church with their aunts and uncles. He cared about "his patients," as he called them. You could feel his passion for their care at staff meetings.

After David retired, he worked for a while as a part-time Disabilities Determination Judge in Baltimore but soon tired of driving across the Bay Bridge and gave up the job. The next time Bruce saw him, he had contracted as an art framer for a waterfowl print shop in Easton—but he soon found that required too much time alone in his garage workshop and ended up with a stack of unused frames and supplies.

While David was moving on with his life, Bruce's private practice increased and he didn't see him for a while. The next Bruce heard, David had suffered a heart attack. He died exercising on his treadmill while trying to stay healthy. When Bruce spoke with Harriett, his widow, he was surprised at what she said. She said he died happy. "He came home the day before," she told Bruce, "smiling and bragging that he'd played the best round of golf in his life."

Bruce knew David played golf once in a while, but he was never close enough to know how passionate he felt about the game. Bruce thinks that if he had asked David what few words or what phrase on his gravestone might summarize what meant the most to him, he might have said, "Husband. Father. Hospital Superintendent. Golfer." And on the back of the stone, he might have had chiseled, "I loved them all."

Psychology is not so much interested in the ultimate meaning of life—the questions of why we're here and who or what put us here. Nonetheless, the psychological research does indicate, at least for some, that passion and overall satisfaction may not be enough for a meaningful life, let alone a flourishing life for all. For some, an idea of how they fit into a picture larger and greater than just themselves is necessary for contentment. For others, the meaning of life is found in achieving something that outlasts them—perhaps something to leave their children, or an artistic legacy, or a trust fund to provide for charitable giving. For some, like Bruce's father, the meaning of life is found in being a good husband and father. For others, meaning derives from striving to reach their inborn potential, whether that be God-given, nature given, or randomly given. Meaning, for those who need and seek it, is both a profound and an everyday matter. It is often part of passion—part of what they love and value that rests at the heart of who they feel they are.

CHAPTER 16

Passionate Progress

Near the end of the movie Serendipity—a story of lost love and missed opportunity—John Cusack's character laments to a friend, "When an ancient Greek died, the Greeks did not write his obituary. They simply asked, 'Did he have passion?'" That suggests that the ancient Greeks, wise in many ways, felt that life didn't amount to much without passion.

If they were right, if passion is the fuel that powers a good life, then it's certainly worth creating and sustaining by savoring, being grateful, and perhaps discovering life's ultimate meaning. It's worth the effort, especially when the effort itself is satisfying. Again, as Socrates, one of those most famous Greeks, said, "The unexamined life is not worth living." When you make an effort to examine what gives you the most joy and satisfaction, in a sense you're following an ancient tradition. And when that examination spurs you to keep pursuing your passions, the result is ongoing satisfaction and the assurance that you're living your most passionate life.

Let's examine this topic further. At the end of this chapter, you'll have a chance to take the Passion Progress Test again to assess how far you've come and what you still want to do.

It Works If You Work It

When your car runs out of gas, sputters, and glides to a stop on the side of the road, should you conclude that the internal combustion engine doesn't work, or that it only works as long as you fill the tank? Similarly, when the medications Lipitor, Ambien, and Viagra lose their effectiveness soon after you stop taking them, should you conclude that those medications are ineffective or that their effectiveness only lasts as long as someone continues to take them?

Those seem like silly questions, but as Sonja Lyubomirsky writes in The How of Happiness (2008), it didn't take long after the end of one of her passion discovery experiments for her subjects to realize that the positive effects only lasted as long as they continued following the procedures. Even the largest effects ebbed without at least occasional practice. On the other hand, Lyubomirsky says that some of her subjects, long after the experiment ended, spontaneously reported that they were pleased and delighted with the continued positive effects, as they had continued to practice after the experiment.

In marriage counseling, it's often the case that couples communicate in a caring, empathetic way in the therapist's office and then relapse after counseling when they stop communicating. It's for this reason that psychologist John Gottman, a primary researcher on marriage counseling, has created what he calls a step-by-step guide to relationship success, the backbone of which is communication skills that are "practiced, practiced, practiced." It's not just knowing what to do," Gottman says, "it's doing it."

The Japanese have a saying that echoes that advice, "If you know something and don't do it, you don't know it."

Major League pitcher Geoff Zahn is a good example of living his passion. Zahn won over a hundred games in the twelve seasons he played for the Dodgers, Cubs, Twins, and Angels. After retiring from the majors, he coached the Pepperdine University team to the regional finals, after which he was recruited to put some wind in the sails of the chronically defeated University of Michigan team. He served at Michigan for six years.

"Our goal is simple," he recalls telling the team when he first met them in 1995. "It's to do something every day to get better as an individual and as a team. Somewhere along the road of life," he went on to say, "I was taught that I never wanted to have any regrets. The worst possible thing that could happen would be to watch a baseball game when you are finished with your career and have to say, 'If I only would have.' It doesn't matter if you are done playing after one year of college or have a long professional career. You want to be able to say when you are done that you passionately gave it all you had."

Zahn now coaches other coaches, telling them if they have a team that applies themselves daily, then they have a team that has a good chance to reach their potential. "Your own passion," he adds, "must turn into your team's passion. It's not always about the final record as much as it is about what you have achieved as a team to move toward improvement and maintaining long-range goals."

Habits for Lifelong Passion

It's one thing to read a book or attend a Passion Discovery or Passion Test workshop and get excited about the lessons you've learned, and even to apply them to good effect. But how do you sustain those results? How do you build upon them instead of letting them go by the wayside?

There are many things you can do. The point of Passion Discovery is not only to instill a temporary passion jolt, but to build lifelong habits that increase and sustain passion. That means doing things that build and grow the neural pathways in your brain that support new life-enhancing habits. Then sustaining passion will become your default mode.

One thing you can do is reread The Passion Principle every once in a while to remind yourself how far you've come and how far you still want to go. Complete the Passion Discovery exercises again every year or so to see what new thoughts or ideas occur to you based on your continuing experience and the changes in your life.

These are the exercises that help you remember what you are passionate about. They prompt you to envision where you can expand your passion into new areas of your life by identifying the underlying passion elements at the root of your most basic needs, desires, and aspirations. Then you're provided the template for passion-based action planning and accountability, which when used will make all the difference in your living your most passionate life.

Getting support for living your passions is key. Look for and build relationships with others who are living their passions full out. Not only will they become inspirational role models for you, but you may become a role model for them in your shared quest to live your very best lives. Choose the best company for that mission and you'll never look back.

Finally, if you slip—if you stop discovering, living, and sustaining passion—recommit and start over again. No matter where you are or how long you've stopped, you will always be building on what you've done before.

Randy's passion for maximum health, energy, and vitality has him up early and at the gym three times a week, with moderate activity in between. He often hears people talk about falling off the wagon with diet or their fitness program. He reminds himself and others that it's not how many times you quit or stop your healthy habits, or any other habits for that matter—it's how many times you start again and stay with it that makes the difference over time.

Building and Stretching Your Passion Muscles

How can you live a life with every minute filled with passion? You can't. But you can live more minutes, hours, and days of passion. In a talk Mihaly Csikszentmihalyi gave to a group of fellow psychologists in Opatija, Mexico, he said, "It is wonderful to see what has happened in such a short period of time in this emerging field of Positive Psychology. What we started has exceeded any expectation we had at the time."

You can never achieve absolute perfection, but you can use what psychology has learned over the past two decades to spark and embed more joy, happiness, and satisfaction in your life. You can do more of what's perfect for you and live your unique passions. You can live a life of greater passion, always "building and stretching your passion muscles."

The Passion Test book refers over and over to a secret that guarantees you can live your most passionate life. It goes like this: "Whenever you are faced with a choice, decision, or opportunity, choose in favor of your passions." We hope that some of the thoughts and exercises in this book will help you do just that.

Here's one way to look at where you are now in your passion journey: Retake the Passion Progress Test.

Passionate Progress Assessment

To see how far you've come, retake the self-assessment you took at the very start (Passion Startup Score in Chapter 1), and then compare your beginning score with your score now.

Don't Agree		Mostly Agree		Strongly Agree		
1	2	3	4	5	6	7

I have put a lot of thought into the personal meaning of passion.

1 2 3 4 5 6 7

I am aware of five specific ways to increase passion in my life.

1 2 3 4 5 6 7

I am confident I can feel more alive and passionate in the future.

1 2 3 4 5 6 7

I am aware of a long list of passions that I could add to my life.

1 2 3 4 5 6 7

I know the procedures to take to define my passions more clearly.

1 2 3 4 5 6 7

I have already begun to increase passion in my life in one or more ways.

1 2 3 4 5 6 7

Ending Passion Score =
(add total numerical scores)

Congratulations! We're cheering you on. Now keep it up!

CHAPTER 17

Spreading Passion Everywhere

This book about discovering, living, and sustaining passion in your life would not be complete without sharing the kind of world we envision once people all over the globe are living and sharing their passions openly and fully—and how to get there.

You've read many stories here about how people have discovered and lived their passions, some despite very challenging circumstances. We've given you some very powerful tools, with many questions to explore, questions whose answers can help you find and bring more passion into your life. And we've substantiated this exploration as having a sound psychological scientific basis.

For those of you who are educators, psychologists, psychiatrists, therapists, social workers, coaches, trainers, or advocates of any kind helping other people—people who are struggling and striving to become more whole, and beyond that to live the life of their dreams—you are truly part of a historical groundswell.

We are in a sweet spot in history where we can harvest all of the theoretical and empirical work done in the last fifty years in what has been called the Human Potential Movement, along with the newer and still emerging field of Positive Psychology. Examples of such work include Abraham Maslow's early work on the hierarchy of needs and peak experiences; psychologist William Schutz's book Joy; and the work of Carl Rogers, grandfather of humanistic psychology.

They and so many other pioneering psychologists and therapists have opened up an entire realm within which to expand our work as facilitators of human fulfillment. Joining these efforts with the experimental models of cognitive psychologist Martin Seligman and others now provides us the equivalent of a swift luge ride into the very heart of human happiness.

In other words, we know what to do. Let's join together and get it done!

Where to Begin

If the world we envision for ourselves is one in which every person we know is engaged with what matters most to them, if every person is tapped into the natural curiosity we all begin with—the creativity and productivity that is an expression of his or her unique identify and gift to the world—where do we begin? With ourselves.

First, those of us dedicated to helping and serving others need to take a close look at whether or not we are serving ourselves. An empty cup serves no one. A half-empty cup is, well, only half full—half of what we could be for ourselves and others. Worse, burnout, health problems, and even death can result from doing the wrong thing—not being aligned with our passions—or doing so much of one thing that it becomes an unhealthy obsession, as we discussed earlier in this book.

Really, what good are we to others if, as the airline flight attendant reminds us, we don't put our own oxygen masks on first?

Sometimes we can wear a professional mask that separates us from our clients, our coworkers, and even our family members. Clear boundaries, identities, and roles are important in both personal and professional life. And yet the masks, roles, or identities we wear sometimes get so hardened that we can forget we have needs of our own. We need to take time out to get clear again about our own passions and to savor life more.

The beauty is that anyone can take a Passion Discovery class and everyone can take the Passion Test. Either of these can be a first but powerful step for realigning people's priorities and life with what they really came here to do and enjoy.

Another step is realizing that no matter where you are, who you are, and what you do, you can become a catalyst for creating a more passionate world simply by modeling passion for others. No speech, no advice, no prescription needed here. When you simply live as though this were the one precious chance you get to live your passions, people around you—the grocery store clerk, the man or woman on the street, the people in your boardroom, or the person in your bedroom—will wonder what's gotten into you and might just say, "What did you do to get there?" or "I'll have what you're having!"

Each One, Teach One

Beyond that, we know that the spread of literacy and other kinds of revolutions have been the result of an "each one, teach one" methodology. So when someone does ask about your apparent zeal for living, you can share the tools and processes that helped you or refer that person to those who helped you gain or regain a passionate sense of life and its many possibilities. All of learning theory supports the idea that when you share and teach someone something, you more firmly learn it and sustain it in your own life.

Have you ever noticed that when you talk about and share your passion with another and ask about the other's passions, you have the most elevated conversations about life? And that you feel naturally energized? Whether at a party or in between meetings, isn't it more fun when people focus on and talk about what they love, rather than falling back into the default option for many—complaining as a way to connect through small talk?

Don't settle for small. Resist that old temptation and redirect the conversation in a natural way to what matters most to people and what turns them on. It can be absolutely transformative in the moment and can sometimes make an enduring impression on those you have those elevated conversations with—maybe even resulting in a turning point in their lives. You never know!

In our relationships and families, as we have shared in our own stories, getting clear about our passions has elevated our conversations even with family members. Parents knowing and supporting their children's passions, as well as sons and daughters seeing parents follow their passions, strengthens families. We've witnessed how the discovery of family members' passions has helped healthy families become healthier and transformed those families struggling to regain a foothold in terms of their connections. A huge piece of resolving family conflict can result from refocusing on what matters most in family life and how family members can better support one another through the life passages that each encounters at his or her particular stage of life development.

Transforming the Lives of Kids and Teens

The Passion Test for Kids and Teens program, which

trains teachers to create the passion-based classroom, gives both the teacher and his or her students a sense of building together the kind of world they most want to live in. We absolutely know that when young people are supported in following their interests and passions, their learning is accelerated on all fronts.

What does it look like when you teach to the passion, not just to the test? Imagine going beyond piecemeal "reform" of our educational system to an entire transformation that more than talks about students' potential—it actually helps students fully develop it. We know that this is an essential part of the making of good citizens and productive, creative, and fulfilled workers, ones that will be passionately engaged in leading their families, communities, and organizations.

There is also a Passion Test facilitator training for children ages nine to fifteen, which supports kids in helping other kids get focused on their passions and what it might take for them to learn and master skills that lead to living those passions. Imagine how their lives would be if the strongest peer pressure young people faced in growing up was the support to engage in what they love to do, learn how to do it, and then do it better and be recognized for their unique expression of themselves.

Passion in Business

There is also a Passion Test for Businesses and Organizations. This robust three-phase program helps any organization or business, from the solo entrepreneur to a company with thousands of employees, get clear about its unique contribution to the world in its signature products and services. The program helps reveal what underlying passions drive that contribution, as well as what everyone in that enterprise values doing that engages their work passions. The result is that the most important business decisions soon become based on the foundation of passion that has been created within that organization.

We love what Chris Attwood, coauthor of The Passion Test and former CEO of several companies, has to say about the bottom line. Chris coined the term passion-based decision making for business, which he recommends in contrast to the normal approach to decision making, primarily based on the company's financial bottom line. In the past decade or two, it's been easier for everyone to see the destructive direction in which solely money-based decisions have taken our economy and our lives. Many of the most successful companies already understand the role of passion in their bottom line and are surging ahead as a result. Imagine helping people achieve their full potential in the workplace by helping people get clear not only about their skills and abilities but also about their work passions, then helping them decide if the enterprise they are already in or considering is the best fit for them—and if not, providing employees with clarity about what most brings them alive and where their contribution can make the most difference.

Imagine all enterprises, whether start-up or restart, tapping into the full human potential of their leaders and associates, not just 20 or 30 percent of their potential. Instead of losing billions of dollars in productivity, as is the case now, those billions could now be recirculated into activities for enhancing the lives of workers, consumers, and citizens.

As organization builders, Randy, Karin, and the business trainers they work with have seen firsthand how these passion-based tools, processes, and programs begin to shift the paradigm by helping create a more compelling vision and a sound basis for making decisions, whether it be about one's own life, one's business, or one's creative endeavor or enterprise of any kind.

WORKSHEETS FOR PASSION DISCOVERY

Current Passion Experiences or Activities (What I currently like and love to do)	Common Passion Elements (Leave this column blank for the moment.)
1.	
2.	
3.	
4.	
(List as many as you can think of.)	

Past Passion Experiences or Activities (What I used to love and like to do)	Common Passion Elements (Leave this column blank for the moment.)
1.	
2.	
3.	
4.	
(List as many as you can think of.)	

Potential Passion Experiences or Activities (What I think I might love and like to do in the future)	Common Passion Elements (Leave this column blank for the moment.)
1.	
2.	
3.	
4.	
(List as many as you can think of.)	

POSSIBLE PASSION ELEMENTS

Here are a few categories of life experience we call Passion Elements. Perhaps you can think of more that fit for you.

_____ Relationships in general or a particular relationship
_____ Achieving or accomplishing something significant
_____ Recognition by others
_____ Quiet satisfaction
_____ Enjoying the beauty of nature
_____ Having profound insights
_____ Spiritual growth and connections
_____ Learning about the world
_____ Learning about myself
_____ Physical activities
_____ Solitude
_____ Team activities
_____ Generating and exploring new ideas
_____ Creating and completing projects
_____ Safety or security
_____ Exercising command or influence
_____ Experiencing beautiful surroundings
_____ Helping or serving others
_____ Self-reliance
_____ Competitive activities
_____ Cooperative activities

WORKSHEET FOR PASSION ACTION PLAN

Use one form for each Passion Element

PASSION ELEMENT (Name or brief description) (Examples: "Exercise" and "Love to be around and care for children")
Times or ways this has happened for me in the past: (Original memory, current specific activity, and/or future potential here) - - - -
Ways or conditions under which this or something like it could happen again for me now or in the future: - - - - -

What I could do to more often find or create these conditions: - - - -
What, either within or outside me, would stop me from creating these conditions? - - - - -
Would I really like to engage in this or something like it more often? (Circle one.) Yes No
In what new or old ways might I engage with this passion element again? - - - -

What small step or steps can I take to gain information or further engage my passion potential in this area? - - - - -
Will I make the personal commitment to take one of these small steps? (Circle one.) Yes No
If "yes," when, where, and how will I take this step?

NOTES AND SELECTED REFERENCES

Introduction

Janet Bray Attwood and Chris Attwood, The Passion Test: The Effortless Path to Discovering Your Life Purpose (New York: Plume, 2008).

Chapter 1: Got Passion?

Malcolm Gladwell, the bestselling author of Blink and The Tipping Point, in reviewing psychologist Dan Gilbert's book Stumbling on Happiness (New York: Vintage Books, 2007).

Dr. Hatcher's 33 Happy Moments asks inmates to list 33 positive experiences from any time in their life, including some that occurred while incarcerated. They also complete a Realistic Life Negative Exercise, in which they are instructed to think of something negative that happened in their life and then describe a lesson they could learn from that experience—a lesson that, if applied, could make their life better in some way.

In the 33 Happy Moments exercise, Hatcher was looking for a potential passion that could turn an inmate around and point him in a more productive direction. Hatcher writes on the national corrections website, "We have now run approximately five groups of five to nine inmates each, and I think we can provide some answers to the question 'Does it work?' First, we have measured positive and negative moods over the course of the class and have in each group found an increase in positive moods and a decrease in negative moods from week to week. Second, we have had individual inmates who told us in no uncertain terms that they 'had never thought like this' and that they found the process to be very helpful to them. Perhaps the best measure is that interest in our group has increased dramatically. From initially having trouble filling the groups, we now have a waiting list."

In the 3 Good Things, subjects were asked to notice three good things that happened to them during the day and then write them down in a journal each night for three weeks. The results, compared to those of a control group who were simply asked to write "something about their life," which resulted in increases in overall happiness and perceived satisfaction.

Chapter 2: What Is Passion, Anyway?

Martin E. P. Seligman, "The President's Address (Annual Report)." American Psychologist 54 (1999): 559–562.

Malcolm Gladwell, the bestselling author of Blink and The Tipping Point, in reviewing psychologist Dan Gilbert's book Stumbling on Happiness (New York: Vintage Books, 2007).

Jonathan Gardner and Andrew J. Oswald. "Money and Mental Wellbeing: A Longitudinal Study of Medium-Sized Lottery Wins," Journal of Health Economics 26, no. 1 (2006): 49–60.

Chapter 3: Passionate YOU!

Christopher Peterson writes in his textbook, A Primer in Positive Psychology (Oxford University Press, 2006), "We all have interests and passions that partially define who we are."

Margaret Wheatley, Leadership and the New Science: Learning About Organization from an Orderly Universe (San Francisco: Berrett-Koehler, 2006).

In one randomly assigned control-group study, Martin Seligman tested "five purported happiness interventions and one plausible control exercise." See Martin E. P. Seligman, T.A. Steen, N. Park, and C. Peterson, "Positive Psychology Progress: Empirical Validation of Interventions," American Psychologist 60, no. 5 (2005), 410–421.

The type of active, energetic aliveness and alertness you will be examining is what psychologists Dr. Gretchen Spreitzer and Christine Porath call "thriving with a vital sense of being alive, passionate, and excited." See Gretchen M. Spreitzer and Robert E. Quinn, A Company of Leaders (San Francisco: Jossey-Bass, 2001).

Christopher Peterson's advice from his A Primer in Positive Psychology (Oxford University Press, 2006).

Chapter 6: Overcoming Obstacles

Sarah Ban Breathnach, Simple Abundance: A Daybook of Comfort and Joy (New York: Grand Central, 2009).

Nancy Shenker, president of ONswitch, a behavior-changing market intelligence site. www.onswitch.co.uk

Meg Grant and Lawrence Grobel, "Sharon Stone Opens

Up," AARP Magazine, January 19, 2012.

Rosabeth Moss Kanter is a Harvard Business School professor and author of Confidence: How Winning Streaks and Losing Streaks Begin and End (Crown Business, 2006).

Jack Canfield is best-selling author of the Chicken Soup for the Soul Series and The Success Principles (New York, William Morrow, 2006)

Psychologist Barbara Fredrickson recounts a traditional Cherokee folk tale. Her book is Positivity: Top-Notch Research Reveals the 3-to-1 Ratio That Will Change Your Life, (Three Rivers Press, 2009)

Ray Bradbury, Fahrenheit 451, (New York: Simon & Schuster, Reprint edition, 2012.)

Chapter 7: Passion versus Obsession

Psychologist Robert Vallerand's video interview on "harmonious passion" versus "obsessive passion." See vallerand.socialpsychology.org.

One study of 191 male and 31 female online game players with a mean age of 23 found that the average number of hours they played per week was twenty-two. See Lafrenière et al., "On the Costs and Benefits of Online Video Gaming: The Role of Passion," Cyberpsychology & Behavior, 2009). The researchers were interested in assessing both the negative and positive consequences of online gaming.

University of Michigan psychology professor Christopher Peterson wrote about what constitutes a passion obsessive. See Christopher Peterson, "The Good Life," Psychology Today, January 7, 2010.

Scott Barry Kaufman, "How to Increase Your Harmonious Passion," Psychology Today, September 26, 2011, https://www.psychologytoday.com/blog/beautiful-minds/201109/how-increase-your-harmonious-passion/

Chapter 8: Really Living What You Love

Todd Kashdan and William Breen, "Materialism and Diminished Well-Being: Experiential Avoidance as a Mediating Mechanism," Journal of Social and Clinical Psychology 26, no. 5 (2007): 521–539.

Chapter 9: Passion Process Advantages

Marci Shimoff and Carol Kline, Happy for No Reason: 7 Steps to Being Happy from the Inside Out (New York: Free Press, 2009).

Mitch Albom, Have a Little Faith: A True Story (New York: Hyperion, 2009)

The nun study is reported in Martin E. P. Seligman, Authentic Happiness: Using the New Positive Psychology to Realize Your Potential for Lasting Fulfillment (New York: Atria Books, 2013).

Chapter 10: Living Passion in Relationships

Psychologist Michael Steger's interview for the Denver Post (Jan 7, 2012)

John R. Buri, How to Love Your Wife (Mustang, OK: Tate, 2006).

Gary Chapman, The Five Love Languages: The Secret to Love That Lasts (Chicago: Northfield, 2005),

John Gottman, The Art and Science of Love: A Workshop for Couples (Seattle: Gottman Institute, 2006).

Psychologists Frank Fincham of Florida State University and Steven Beach of the University of Georgia studied the connection between forgiveness and the quality of marital life in a sample of ninety-one couples over a twelve-month period. See Frank Fincham and Steven R. Beach, "Forgiveness and Marital Quality: Precursor or Consequence in Well-Established Relationships," Journal of Positive Psychology 2, no. 4, (2007): 260–268.

John Gottman's "bad events are so much stronger than good ones that the good must far outnumber the bad in order to prevail." See Gottman, The Art and Science of Love.

Bruce Feiler, The Council of Dads: My Daughters, My Illness, and the Men Who Could Be Me (New York: William Morrow, 2010).

Chapter 11: Passion for Work

French chef, author, and television personality Eric Ripert's interview for Tricycle Magazine (Winter, 2011)

Shakti Gawain, Creative Visualization (New World Library, 2002).

Charles Darwin, On the Origin of Species,1859.

Lance Secretan, Inspirational Leadership (Secretan, 2003).

Jonathan Haidt, The Happiness Hypothesis (Basic Books, 2006)

Denice Kronau, Falling in Love with Work: A Practical Guide to Igniting Your Passion for Your Career (Wheatmark, 2011).

Christopher Peterson et al., "Classifying and Measuring Strengths of Character," in Oxford Handbook of Positive Psychology, eds. S. J. Lopez and C. R. Snyder (New York: Oxford University Press, 2009): 25–33.

Nicholas Hall, January 6, 2007 blog titled "Positive Psychology and Person-Job Fit."

Chapter 12: Savoring

Bill and Melinda Gates Foundation,

www.gatesfoundation.org

Research psychologists Christopher Peterson and Nansook Park, Positive Psychology Resources 2012, University of Michigan Ann Arbor, MI.

Satoshi Shimai, "Happy People Become Happier through Kindness: A Counting Kindnesses Intervention," Journal of Happiness Studies 7, no. 3 (2006): 361–375, http://link.springer.com/article/10.1007/s10902-005-3650-z/

German neurologist Kurt Goldstein's 1942 studies are reported in James Smith, Emotional Intelligence: What You Need to Know (Dayboro, Australia: Emereo, 2012).

Abraham H. Maslow, A Theory of Human Motivation, (Mansfield Center, CT: Martino Fine Books, 2013)

Sherrie Bourg Carter, High-Octane Women: How Superachievers Can Avoid Burnout (Amherst, NY: Prometheus Books, 2010)

Susan Biali, Live a Life You Love, (Beaufort Books, 2011)

Fred Bryant, Savoring: A New Model of Positive Experience, (Psychology Press, 2006)

Externalizer/Internalizer is part of John Gittinger's original Personality Assessment System found at http://www.pasf.org/gitt.htm

Chapter 13: Being in Flow

Flow is described in detail in Mihaly Csikszentmihalyi, Flow: The Psychology of Optimal Experience (New York: Harper Perennial, 2008)

Quotes on time are from Hsiang Chen, Rolf T. Wigand, and Michael Sanford Nilan, "Exploring Web Users' Optimal Flow Experiences," Information Technology & People 13, no. 4 (2000): 263–281.

De Manzano states that, "Expert performance is commonly accompanied by a subjective state of optimal experience called 'flow.' Previous research has shown positive correlations between flow and quality of performance and suggests that flow may function as a reward signal that promotes practice." See Orjan de Manzano, Tores Theorell, Laszlo Harmat, and Frederik Ullen, "The Psychophysiology of Flow During Piano Playing," Journal of Emotion 10, no. 3 (2010): 301–311.

The Falko Rheinberg and Stefan Engeser quote, "one feels both optimally challenged and confident that everything is under control," is from "Flow, Performance and Moderators of Challenge-Skill Balance," Motivation and Emotion 32, no. 3 (2008): 158–172.

Sue Halpern, Four Wings and a Prayer (New York: Vintage, 2002)

In her own study of flow, sports psychologist Susan Jackson interviewed sixteen champion figure skaters who won national titles between 1985 and 1990. See S. A. Jackson, "Toward A Conceptual Understanding of The Flow Experience in Elite Athletes," Research Quarterly for Exercise and Sport 67, no. 1 (1996): 76–90.

Psychologist Brennan Payne set out to investigate flow in older adults. He studied 197 adults ages 60 to 94 residing in an adult community. See Brennan R. Payne, Joshua J. Jackson, Soo Rim Noh, and Elizabeth A. L. Stine Morrow, "In the Zone: Flow State and Cognition in Older Adults," Psychology and Aging 26, no. 3 (2011): 738–743.

Csikszentmihalyi wrote on the strategies that generate flow. See Mihaly Csikszentmihalyi, Flow: The Psychology of Optimal Experience (New York: Harper Perennial, 2008).

Chapter 14: Being in Gratitude

Dale Chihuly says he's been passionate about the color and properties of glass ever since childhood and feels grateful every day that he is able to work in a medium he loves. He once said so in an online interview on the Academy of Achievement website (www.achievement.org)

In one study conducted at the University of California, Robert Emmons examined sixty-five adults suffering from congenital or adult-onset neuromuscular disease. Each participant was assigned the task of noticing and then listing daily events for which he or she felt grateful. Emmons then compared the results with two control groups assigned to other writing tasks. See Robert A. Emmons and Michael E. McCullough, "Counting Blessings versus Burdens: An Experimental Investigation of Gratitude and Subjective Well-Being in Daily Life," Journal of Personality and Social Psychology 84, no. 2 (2003): 377–389.

In one study, Tiffany A. Ito and Jeff Larsen measured the brainwaves of subjects who viewed a series of positive, negative, and neutral pictures. See Tiffany A. Ito, Jeff T. Larsen, Kyle Smith, and John T. Cacioppo, "Negative Information Weighs More Heavily on the Brain: The Negativity Bias in Evaluative Categorizations," Journal of Personality and Social Psychology 75, no. 4 (1998): 887–900.

In their Evolutionary Psychology: A Primer (Santa Barbara, CA: Center for Evolutionary Psychology, 1997), Leda Cosmides and John Tooby summarize three principal reasons for an evolutionary bias toward negativity.

Roy Baumeister and Ellen Bratslavsky summed up the evidence for a negative human bias in the landmark article "Bad Is Stronger Than Good," Review of General Psychology 5, no. 4 (2001): 323–370.

Here is a partial list of some of the psychological studies on gratitude:

STUDY	SAMPLE GROUP	INSTRUCTIONS	RESULT
Emmons and McCullough (2003) Study 1	Sixty-five young adults	For each of 10 weeks, list up to 5 things for which to be grateful.	Increased gratitude, hours exercising, and life satisfaction.
Emmons and	Seventy young	Each day for 2 weeks, list up to	Increased gratitude

McCullough (2003) Study 2	adults	five things for which to be grateful.	and positive affect.

Emmons and McCullough (2003) Study 2	Seventy young adults	Each day for 2 weeks, list up to five things for which to be grateful.	Increased providing emotional support. Decreased negative affect.
Watkins et al. (2003)	One hundred and four young adults	List things done over the previous summer that they felt grateful for.	Significantly increased positive affect and decreased negative affect.
Lyubomirsky, Tkach, and Sheldon (2004)	College students	Think about things they are grateful for once a week for 6 weeks.	Increases in measured sense of well-being.
Froh et al. (2008)	Forty-four early adolescents in a school setting	Each day for 2 weeks, list up to 5 things for which to be grateful.	Decreased negative affect. Increased school satisfaction.
Geraghty Et all.	Adult Community	Kept a 2-week Gratitude diary	Better body Satisfaction.

Study 1 (2011)	sample of 40 interent adults	List 6 things each day.	

Chart Information from Alex M Wood, Jeffrey J. Froh, and Adam W. A. Geraghty, "Gratitude and Well-Being," Clinical Psychology Review 30, no 7 (2010): 890–905.

Chapter 15: Meaning and Passion

Christopher Peterson and Nansook Park concluded that the pursuit of meaning was "much more predictive of life satisfaction than the pursuit of pleasure." See Christopher Peterson, Nansook Park, and Martin E. P. Seligman, Greater Strengths of Character and Recovery from Illness," The Journal of Positive Psychology 1, no. 1 (2006): 17–26.

Martin E. P. Seligman, Authentic Happiness: Using the New Positive Psychology to Realize Your Potential for Lasting Fulfillment (New York: Atria Books, 2013).

Martin E. P. Seligman, Flourish: A Visionary New Understanding of Happiness and Well-Being (New York: Free Press, 2011).

Shigehiro Oishi and Selin Kesebir define the search of meaning as "the strength, intensity, and activity of someone's desire and efforts to establish and/or augment their understanding of the significance and purpose of their lives." See Michael F. Steger, Shigehiro Oishi, and Selin Kesebir, "Is a Life Without Meaning Satisfying? The Moderating Role of the Search for Meaning in Satisfaction with Life Judgments," The Journal of Positive Psychology 6, no. 3 (2011): 173–180.

Mihaly Csikszentmihalyi wrote, "A good life consists of more than simply the totality of enjoyable experiences. It must also have a meaningful pattern, a trajectory of growth that results in the development of increasing emotional, cognitive, and social complexity." See Mihaly Csikszentmihalyi, Good Business: Leadership, Flow, and the Making of Meaning (New York: Penguin, 2003).

Jane Fonda, Prime Time (New York: Random House, 2011).

Psychologist and researcher Michael Steger writes in Psychology Today (April, 2009).

Chapter 16: Passionate Progress

Sonja Lyubomirsky, The How of Happiness (New York: Penguin, 2008).

Mihaly Csikszentmihalyi, "The Promise of Positive Psychology," Psychological Topics 18, no. 2 (2009): 203–211.

Chapter 17: Spreading Passion Everywhere

William Schutz, Joy: Expanding Human Awareness (New York: Grove Press, 1967).

The Passion Principle Project

Be part of something big. Inspire others while you inspire yourself. Share your passion journey. Where did you begin and how did you get from where you began to where you are now? What obstacles stood in your path and how did you overcome them? What did you learn from reading The Passion Principle and how did you put it into practice? Help others find their passion by showing them what worked for you.

Share your story online—using your name or a pseudonym—and be willing to be part of a forthcoming follow-up book. Describe who you are and tell a little about yourself, then send your story in as much detail as you can. Thanks so much for being part of this.

Send your story to:

www.quantumleapcoaching.org.

About the Authors

Bruce Hutchison, PhD, is a clinical psychologist, graduate school instructor, and international workshop presenter.

Randy Crutcher, EdD, is a personal and professional development coach, trainer, facilitator, and consultant for teams and organizations. For more information, you can visit www.quantumleapcoaching.org

Made in the USA
Lexington, KY
20 November 2019